Praise For
A Life That Works

If you're interested in a book full of practical wisdom for your everyday life, this book's for you! Bruce writes the way he speaks-every page is chock full of authentic, down-to-earth, nonboring stories and truths. I've known Bruce for 40 years and he's the real deal! Grab a cup of coffee and your favorite armchair because you won't be able to put this book down (except for contemplation).

Peter J. Iliyn
Former North American Director-Youth With A Mission

A LIFE *that* WORKS

Deep Wisdom For a Changing World

BRUCE STEFANIK

STORY ⫸ CHORUS

To Linda.

My faithful other half, and my greatest fan all these years.

To Jacob and Heather, David and Brittanie.

I am so proud of you. You inspire me to be better.

Luke, you keep me laughing and thinking all the time.

Don't forget who loves you most. Sue and Dave, thank you

for introducing me to the One who changed everything.

Table of Contents

TABLE OF CONTENTS

CHAPTER ONE

Who Doesn't Want a Life That Works?

"The Christian ideal has not been tried and found wanting. It has been found difficult; and left untried."

– G.K. Chesterton, *What's Wrong with the World*

"Hold on to instruction, do not let it go; guard it well, for it is your life."

– Proverbs 4:13

A young man named John sat in my office. It should have been the happiest time of his life. He was engaged to a wonderful woman, about to get married. From the outside, John had a promising life. But as he began to share with me, it was clear nothing in his life seemed to be working.

I was new to ministry in the States, serving as a staff pastor. And, like most such meetings, the small talk at the start didn't fool me. No one asks for a meeting with a pastor for chit-chat.

When the pleasantries found a lull, I asked, "So what's going on, John?"

His eyes clouded with despair. I could tell he was hurting. He began to unpack all the problems in his life, problems that filled every major category we experience, from relationships to finances to personal shame.

The fights between him and his fiancé were escalating, and the conflict was really concerning him. He still lived with his parents and was feeling the pinch of not having the freedom he should have experienced as an independent adult. In addition to that, John's finances were in shambles, with towering credit card debt about to crush him—debt he'd be bringing into his new marriage, which would add stress right from the start.

I listened without interrupting. I had a feeling what was coming next.

John paused, stumbling for words. His head ducked down, and he looked at his hands that were clenched in his lap.

"I am really struggling with pornography," he said. It was clear he was ashamed. It was also clear he felt like a failure in nearly every other area of his life, as well. This young guy full of potential and promise was at a breaking point.

"Pastor Bruce, what do I do?" he asked.

Instead of giving him some key Bible verses or a pep talk about self-control, I asked him a question in return. I have always been fascinated by how Jesus repeatedly asked people questions instead of giving them obvious answers to their problems.

"John, does the Jesus you believe in have a place in your life?"

He'd said *a lot* about *a whole lotta* things. But for a Christian guy, a regular walk with Jesus hadn't come up at all.

John looked confused. "You mean, in my *everyday* life?"

I nodded as I thought to myself, *"Isn't that where all your problems are?"* I then asked. "How does your walk with Jesus influence your daily life?"

He seemed completely taken aback. I could tell by his reaction he'd never given that idea much thought. How many of us do think about how our walk with Jesus influences our daily lives at any age? Like so many people I've talked to in similar difficulties, John was living a compartmentalized life. John had things figured out on Sundays when everything seemed to be working; but when Monday rolled around, all of his problems came crashing back in.

John and I met several more times in later years. He did well, but there were some deep patterns that had to be addressed. Still that first meeting sticks with me decades after he walked out the door. I've remembered that conversation, not because John was unique, but because he was typical.

AN EVERYDAY KIND OF FAITH

Keeping Jesus from influencing every area of our everyday lives seems like a factory setting.

We tuck our faith into its Sunday morning compartment—and Wednesday night if we're extra special. But the rest of the week? That's ours. Now it could be that we're selfish and uninterested in what God has to say to us in the different seasons and areas of our lives. However, I think the bigger reason is because we're simply used to working things out on our own.

But that's where the Book of Proverbs meets us—at the end of our know-how. Even though it's a few thousand years old, its wisdom isn't restricted to a particular culture or time period. It is ageless. Limitless. And always relevant. When I look at the ways of Jesus and what He spoke about, the truth and the wisdom of His words could apply to everyone, whether they were a blind beggar, a broken woman, or the rich elite.

Jesus made it clear that the Gospel was for everyone because we all share a common malady. We *all* have sinned and fallen short of the mark, according to Romans 3:23, so that puts us all in the same boat together. However, just as we share the same problem, the truth that sets us free is available to "whosoever will" with no exceptions.

We can't say that same piece of wisdom didn't apply to us, nor could we say that it was too complicated to understand. Jesus made the Gospel accessible to all ages, making a point to say that childlike faith was necessary (Matthew 18:4). Yet childlike faith isn't the same as living a childish life. The mark of dangerous immaturity is thinking that we are smart enough or sophisticated enough to live above the timeless principles found in God's Word.

So, how do we make sure the Gospel seeps and flows into every nook and cranny of our lives? Can we actually put it into action during the week?

Proverbs, like other parts of God's Word, is descriptive rather than prescriptive. It contains a series of sayings that cover a broad range of topics. It talks a lot about patterns that build healthy relationships and a life that works. A lot of the Proverbs seem to have been written from the perspective of a father trying to impart wisdom to a young man, by observing human behavior at work. We stumble when we read Scripture as always prescriptive (e.g. God condones slavery) rather than descriptive (e.g. slavery existed, and this is how God worked despite it).

I've been in love with Proverbs, a nearly 3,000-year-old book, for over 30 years. Its timeless principles will stand for another 3,000 years, and I want to see its wisdom put into action in daily lives.

To do that, we have to see that it's a book of wisdom, not formulas.

WISDOM FOR THE JOURNEY

Wisdom, someone once said, is "the ability to see around the corner." Wouldn't that be a wonderful superpower to have as you go through life?

It's not simply about gathering lots of information. It's not making decisions based on gut feelings. It's not simply relying on the advice of friends. Those things might work occasionally (and definitely might not), but wisdom is something uniquely different. Wisdom is a timely application of knowledge that produces life-giving results.

Wisdom's ability to indicate where our decisions might land us isn't the same as predicting the future. We'd like to be able to predict the future because many of us prefer a transactional way of life. Do this, get this. It's simple and easy.

The problem is we do not live in a morally neutral universe. We may not go looking for trouble, but sometimes trouble comes looking for us. And it's there we need to know how to choose in such a way that our lives are enriched rather than diminished.

The first nine chapters in Proverbs describe Lady Wisdom and Folly as if they were different personalities both beckoning for our attention. The rest seems like a mashup of sayings. But if we try to make them into formulas, they don't work. They function as patterns.

Whenever I'm teaching Proverbs, I'll often ask those who are younger than 30 to raise their hands. "Here is one thing I think I know about you," I tell them. "Your car insurance is most likely costing you more than mine."

Why is that? Because after insurance companies have run the numbers and see the patterns, they come to a simple conclusion. Younger drivers get into more accidents. Why would that be? Because in general, they have less experience behind the wheel coupled with a high level of confidence, making for a potentially dangerous combination. The companies know which way younger drivers lean.

"I am confident I can juggle texting and driving."

"Speed limits do not apply to me."

"I can handle these road conditions."

Of course, it is not a crime to be young, but it does come with some liabilities. The first stage of learning is the most vulnerable because it's at this stage that you don't even know what you don't know! This is why we tell our toddlers to hold our hands when walking through a busy parking lot. They have no framework to understand the potential danger of moving cars. Trust us, we tell them. I am looking out for your good.

The book of Proverbs has 31 chapters. Unlike all the others, only chapter seven has a story; and it speaks to the importance of observing and understanding patterns.

The writer is watching a drama unfold outside his window. He can see the city street below. Walking there is a young man who, we're told, was simple and without understanding. This doesn't mean he was stupid or even that he was inclined to evil. It means he was inexperienced and undecided in how he would live, and he was unaware that he was in a vulnerable position.

A beautiful and sensual woman comes out of her home, positioning herself on the street corner. She's holding all the cards, planning to take advantage of what seems to be an easy catch. She promises the young man everything. She appeals to his carnal instincts and assures him that this is an opportunity not to be missed. It's not long before she persuades the young man, and the writer watches as he follows her off to a fate that he has not discerned. The visual imagery is graphic; "He followed her like an ox going to the slaughter!"

And the man watching the scene unfold outside his window turns to his young sons to interpret for them what just took place. "My sons, listen to me," he says. "Pay attention to what is going on here and more importantly pay attention to people who want access to your heart!" He warns them about the deadly combination of a seductive woman and a naive young man. "Do not let your heart turn to her ways or stray into her paths. Many are the victims she has brought down" (Proverbs 7:25–26).

The point of the story is not to pin blame entirely on the woman or the man but to paint a picture of human nature in action. They were both equally lost to God and themselves.

Whenever a serious accident takes place, investigators will often attempt to analyze the details of the incident to determine what was happening as the tragedy unfolded. They are trying to trace back the events to the core factors that led to the crash. In Proverbs 7, watching from a higher vantage point, there was certainly a slow train wreck taking place in the young man's life—but what caused it?

He was living life according to an unseen and undiscerned pattern, which he had not identified beforehand and didn't see at work before it was too late.

Many of our patterns come from what we've experienced, from strategies that have developed out of previous and oftentimes unresolved issues in our lives. Webster describes *instinct* as *"behavior that is mediated by reactions below the conscious level."* Running on instinct can certainly help us in some situations where action is required, and we don't have enough time or information to process what is happening. However, in other contexts, it impairs our judgment or ability to discern what is truly going on in the greater scheme of things. Have you ever noticed yourself reacting to someone in a way that seemed out of proportion to the circumstance? A strong reaction to an authority figure or the opposite sex? Or a burst of anger or defensiveness that seemed to come out of nowhere? Oftentimes in a marriage counseling situation that involves a conflict, it is obvious that each party has a strong opinion about who or what is right or wrong; and they find themselves at an impasse. It's there that we try to encourage the couple to see a third opinion they might consider, which would be God's opinion! What wisdom might He bring to this picture to help us both see this differently and provide a way forward? God's vantage point from above it all can prove to be a source of great wisdom. Perhaps at that moment, we can begin to understand that we don't simply have a marriage problem. We have a faith problem that is slow to acknowledge or welcome God's counsel.

One time as I was teaching a group of missionaries in a training session overseas, a young man approached me after the class and asked to speak with me privately. I could sense that he was agitated about something. As he spoke, he proceeded to inform me that it was unbearable to listen to me or even remain in the classroom as I taught.

I was a little taken aback, since I'd never met him before that morning's session, and so I asked him to help me understand what I had done to provoke such a strong reaction. At first, he struggled to put it into words, but he then simply blurted out that I vividly reminded him of his father. It wasn't about what I was saying. Rather it was my tone of voice and my teaching style that triggered his instinct to block me out. It was like stepping on an emotional landmine. Neither of us had any idea it was there until I stepped on it and he reacted, and it was very real to him regardless of my intentions.

Have you ever experienced a situation where the reaction seems wildly out of proportion to the offense? Because of the patterns in our life, we often find ourselves unconsciously leaning in certain directions.

In commenting on Proverbs 7, the author Eugene Peterson pointed out how the woman was able to entice the young man to lean towards her. Once she'd accomplished that, the rest was easy. Just like the technique used in certain martial arts, getting your opponent to lean puts them off-balance and makes them easier to topple.

The young man in Proverbs 7 was easy prey. He was someone who was alone and naive, unaware that he was not operating in a morally neutral universe, unaware that there might be someone hunting for his soul. Historically the Church has held fast to the doctrine that the world, the flesh, and the devil are all forces that we need to reckon with because of their potential to influence us to lean in certain ways. And then we find ourselves easily tipping in a direction that we did not intend.

Our enemy, who Jesus described as "the father of lies," is watching to see which way we're leaning. He can't read our mind, but I believe he can observe our patterns. He knows which lies have influenced our past, and he repackages them to try to influence our futures. Talk to just about anybody who has done the hard work of coming out of addictions, and they will tell you that it was identifying and dealing with destructive patterns of thoughts and actions that led to their freedom and transformation.

What could have saved that young man in Proverbs 7?

Perhaps being willing to slow down and ask some questions of a wiser, more experienced voice? What about having a developed self-awareness of his leanings and tendencies? Or having a history of stories to draw on that would help him be able to spot the pattern before it pulled him in? Of course, none of those worked in his circumstance because he was a man who was alone and who chose to be true to his feelings in the moment.

Which way do you find yourself leaning in critical or anxious times? What does the pattern of giving in to temptation look like? Recovery groups wisely frame the question as, "When you're hungry, angry, lonely, or tired, where do you find yourself tempted to lean?" For some it could be as relatively harmless as comfort food or a long nap, but for others it is the dangerous gravitation towards self-pity, isolation, or self-indulgence of some kind. It was Socrates that gave us the philosophical maxim "To know thyself is the beginning of wisdom." That is helpful advice, but are we really able to accomplish that effectively in our own strength? This is where we need a wise and discerning guide who knows the way well. An outfitter who is not simply trying to sell you expensive equipment to bolster your sense of security, but someone who actually has your best interests in mind.

VALUE MATTERS

In Proverbs 3:15–16 we read that wisdom is, "More precious than rubies; nothing you desire can compare with her. Long life is in her right hand; in her left hand are riches and honor. Happy is the man who finds wisdom and gains understanding." We nod our head in agreement because happiness is the overarching goal, right?

Proverbs goes on to tell us all the wonderful things that come with wisdom. She promises a prosperous and full life that can only be found by coming into agreement with the idea that wisdom is actually better than riches.

But how do we actually implement that reality in our day-to-day existence? It has been my observation that the defining mark of a disciple begins with their ability to discern true value. Whether we can perceive true value functions like an unseen, internal compass that informs our life decisions, interprets our suffering, and anchors our losses and hopes.

Whenever I get a chance to teach Proverbs, I often tell a story to illustrate this point.

Let's say I'm on stage and Jimmy, who's five, is in the audience. He hasn't lived a lot of life yet, but he has some experiences under his belt and is your typical boy.

"Jimmy, come up on the stage. I want you to help me out here," I say.

He bounces up the stairs, excited to participate.

"Jimmy, I have two things behind my back, one in each of my hands," I tell him. "You get to take one of them home because I'm going to give it to you."

Jimmy is immediately intrigued.

"Now, I am going to show them to you one at a time," I explain, "and then you'll get to choose which one you want. You're totally free to choose, but you can only have one of the two."

Jimmy is practically jumping up and down because he knows he's going to get a prize. It has the feel of being on the game show *Let's Make a Deal*.

I pull one hand out and there he sees a one-pound bar of rich chocolate in my palm.

"Chocolate!" he says excitedly. He is familiar with what it is. He knows he likes it. His desires kick in and he begins to imagine just how long that huge bar of chocolate will last him.

The crowd calls out trying to help him now, "Jimmy, take the chocolate!" They can see how much he wants it.

"No, no, no, wait Jimmy," I say, holding him back a bit. "Before you make a decision you need to see what's in my other hand."

"Okay, well, what is it?" he asks impatiently, eyes on the chocolate, mouth salivating.

I pull out my other hand. There's a piece of paper in it, a little three-by-six-inch thin sheet of paper. It's a check written to Jimmy for $1000.

"Now you've seen both," I say. Turning to the audience, I tell them about the check made out to Jimmy. The audience is screaming all kinds of things. Jimmy is confused, eyes darting back to the chocolate.

At that point, when I'm telling this story, I ask people how they think it will end. "If you were betting on this outcome, how many of you think Jimmy is going to take the chocolate?"

Most raise their hands. How do we know that?

It's not because Jimmy is evil or foolish. It's not because chocolate is sinful. It's because he's simply uninformed. I would expect him to reach for the chocolate. I would be shocked if he didn't. Youthfulness or even ignorance isn't a sin, but it *is* a fact of life and, in this case, impairs his ability to walk away with the better thing.

What do we adults know that perhaps Jimmy doesn't? That he could delay that instant gratification, take the check to the bank, and buy a whole truckload of chocolate! So, I point it out. "Jimmy did not yet have the tools to discern real value, and so he went home with a chocolate bar and left $1000 on the table."

Everyone nods their head and chuckles, but then we go to a more real life example.

"Ladies, let's say we're in a premarital coaching session, and your fiancé, Bob, is sitting across from me. Wanting to help them discover what governs their decision-making process, I offer him the same scenario I presented to our young friend Jimmy, the check or the chocolate. What happens if in that moment Bob hesitates? What if he is genuinely struggling to make a decision here? Perhaps he even voices a comment about that being his favorite brand of chocolate?"

As his future wife, there might be some alarm bells going off in your head. At this point in the illustration, there might be some indications that he is not ready to be engaged to anyone.

It may sound like a silly exercise, but here's my point. If Bob is even casually considering taking the chocolate, if he can't delay gratification, if he struggles to discern what has greater value in this circumstance, what might that mean for your marriage when far more important decisions are on the line? Will he be there for your children when they need him, or will he choose to hang out with his buddies? If you encounter some serious turbulence in your relationship, will he stick it out and learn to persevere, or will he go find someone else? A chocolate bar is worth a chuckle, but the inability to discern value can have serious implications.

Discerning value is about choosing the best thing, not necessarily the easiest thing.

Jimmy and the chocolate bar is a silly illustration, yes, but people make terrible decisions all the time that are as mind-boggling as what Jimmy did. I often see the outcome when good people who made poor decisions end up in my office, broken and struggling.

When you're younger, like Jimmy, you're vulnerable because you simply don't have the perspective that comes from life experiences. That's why God designed children to be raised alongside stable and seasoned parents. Not perfect parents, but people who have experienced some measure of life and learned what does or does not work! As you age, being innocent or naive should no longer be an excuse. And perhaps worse, these chronically bad decisions indicate that something deeper is going on. Proverbs describes the key to life's wisdom as having the "fear of the Lord."

> DISCERNING VALUE IS ABOUT CHOOSING THE BEST THING, NOT NECESSARILY THE EASIEST THING.

Having the fear of God, among other things, means that we acknowledge who we are dealing with. That the God of the universe, whose eyes are in every place beholding both the good and the evil, has unlimited capacity to help us make wise and loving decisions! He not only sees what we do, but He also designed us to be in a relationship with Him so we don't have to make critical decisions alone. When we're alone, we are all vulnerable to faulty or short sighted thinking. I never cease to be amazed at how people in positions of significant power and authority or with extensive education are capable of making very poor and painful life decisions.

Foolishness is no respecter of persons. It's an equal-opportunity stumbling block. As believers, we affirm that the grace of Jesus has the power to cover every sin; but have you noticed that, in spite of deep forgiveness, we will, along with others, sometimes still deal with the consequences of bad or selfish choices?

An interesting fact about icebergs: as large as they may appear on the surface, ninety percent of their mass is under the surface. When people tell me they are struggling with a particular problem, I often have to help them discover where the real problem lies. Many times, we find that what they are struggling with is really a symptom of a deeper issue. Perhaps it's not just a lust problem or a marriage problem or a bad habit problem. Maybe, at its core, it's a faith problem.

It's a faith problem because you're making decisions that show you don't really believe in your heart that God is present with you everywhere, at all times, and that He has wisdom for any situation or circumstance. What we believe in our hearts to be of greatest value will operate like an invisible internal compass that affects how and why we choose certain directions. Despite what the world tells us, this side of heaven, the most valuable treasure we can acquire is wisdom from on high.

YOU MUST BE ABLE TO DISCERN TRUTH

Two of the most important questions we will ever ask are "what is true?" and "why does it matter?" The writer of Psalm 115 said in verse 8 that we become like the idols we fashion or trust (Psalm 115:8). If my idol is shaped into my image, my image won't allow for disappointment and suffering. We indulge every whim, and I become the center of my universe.

Patrick Morely, founder of Man in the Mirror ministries, makes a distinction in his sermon *What We Learn From Wise Men* pointing out that there's a god we want and there's a God who is, but they might not be the same God. Real change in our life happens when we start seeking the God who actually is, instead of the god we want.

Real change begins to happen when we say no to our false ideas about God and say yes to the God who is, even though it might cause some discomfort and suffering. The Biblical term for that practice is called "repentance" to change the way I think about a matter.

Fantasy is firmly embedded in our current culture. It has become not just a place to escape to on occasion, but for many it's also a place where people find themselves operating for extended periods of time. The rising tide of fake news, AI technology, virtual reality, deep fake media, and unlimited pornography at our fingertips have all helped create a world where the lines are dangerously blurred between what is real and what is not. The problem here is that those artificial worlds are not merely cheap counterfeits, but rather deliberate and dangerous counterfeits that have a desired end in mind.

Imagine that I want to have a lot of money and nice things, but I don't really want to work for it. So, I go home and start making fake money out of green construction paper, gluing my own photo to the center of the fake bill. I write "$20" in each corner, and I walk into the store to buy a one-dollar cookie.

I don't really want the cookie. I just want the $19 change.

At just a glance, the clerk behind the counter would say, "Um, sir, this is a joke, right?" Clearly, my counterfeit money is fake, as if a preschooler made it.

But what happens if I'm actually good at counterfeiting, using high-end printers and paper and inks to create money that looks and feels like the real thing? I go in, buy that cookie, the clerk doesn't catch it, and I walk out $19 richer than when I went in.

Both bills were fake. Both were equally worthless pieces of paper. But one of those bills was dangerous. My downfall didn't come through the obvious fake. It was the dangerous counterfeit, the one that seemed real, that hooked me in.

The main weapon our enemy uses against us is the lie. Jesus described our adversary as the father of lies and said that lies are his native language. He is very good at lying, not clumsy like the childish $20 bill. The counterfeit that looks and smells like the real thing is still worthless—all counterfeits are worthless—but the difference is that it's *dangerous*. Why?

Because the counterfeit only has power over you if you take it. The moment the money was received, the lie was empowered. There are lots of untruths out there; but the moment you believe a particular lie, you give it power to run its course. Some are relatively harmless. "You better take that couch home today. This sale will be your last chance for that price." Some are far more serious and have far reaching effects.

"That relationship over there would be better and easier. No need to fight for my marriage."

"You will never amount to anything."

And the big one in the garden that started it all …

"Don't trust God; trust yourself." '

These thoughts might go through your head and tempt you; but it's the moment you put them in the till, so to speak, that you give them authority over you. A lie's power is found in the combination of demonic influence and human decision. Our enemy speaks it and we believe it.

Any thought, be it good or bad, played often enough in our minds becomes an action that, repeated over and over, becomes a habit that shapes a lifestyle. The danger is that once a lie has found an open door, what started out as a momentary decision of pleasure or relief potentially becomes a pattern that dominates your life. People tell me all the time that they can't live without their addiction, or that they are prone to anger or depression, or they are overpowered by insecurity or some unexplainable fear. They struggle to discern what's true, and it seems like a stronghold has been created in their life.

Quite often, we have heard repentance explained as turning around and going in a different direction, simply changing movement and action. I think that better describes the fruit of repentance. The Greek word it comes from is *metanoia*, meaning to change how you think.

We talk about repentance calling on people to stop doing something, but they will never stop doing something until they change the way they think about what they are doing! In Romans 12:2, we're told it's the renewing of the mind that matters, not the renewing of our habits.

The problem isn't the habit we keep quitting, it's the lie we haven't stopped believing. Until we change how we think about our relationship to the lie, change doesn't come. Pastor and author John Piper has made it his life message to make the point that God is most glorified when we are most satisfied in Him.

Not in momentary pleasures. Not in idols. Not in little gods. But in God, who is Truth. I will never find victory over the sin problem in my life unless I dig a deeper well of love for God.

The shift in our thinking that must occur to make that happen can't be brought about simply with good intentions or the right information or even acquiring more knowledge. It requires the Holy Spirit to change the desires that rule us. Psalm 37:4 tells us that when we delight in God, He gives us the desires of our hearts. We need to realize that God changes us so that our heart desires what is true and good. This is what C.S. Lewis was referring to when he said in *The Weight of Glory*:

"It would seem that Our Lord finds our desires not too strong, but too weak. We are half-hearted creatures, fooling about with drink and sex and ambition when infinite joy is offered us, like an ignorant child who wants to go on making mud pies in a slum because he cannot imagine what is meant by the offer of a holiday at the sea. We are far too easily pleased."

DON'T YOU WANT TO KNOW THE AUTHOR?

"Wow, you've been married 35 years?!" I said to a couple I had recently met. Considering the divorce rates in our culture, that was impressive. So then I made an assumption. "Are you believers?"

"No," they told me.

After more conversation, I realized that even though they weren't followers of Christ, they had lived those years with each other while actually applying principles found in the Word of God! This does not negate in any way our need for the cross of Christ in our lives, nor does it earn our salvation. It simply shows that the principles work because that's how God framed His world to operate! They are reaping the benefits of God's common grace offered to all people to enjoy. Telling the truth to each other, forgiving one another, practicing humility, and honoring one another are all ideas that began in the heart of God.

I've read about studies in which people who have been married a long time shared their secrets of a long-lasting relationship. Not all the people in the study were Christians, but their answers were surprisingly similar.

"We refused to go to bed angry."

"We work at believing the best about each other."

"We pick our battles wisely."

They are taking the wisdom that's been there through generations and applying it to their everyday lives, regardless of where it originated. Many of us have done the same, aligning our lives on aphorisms. These are simply the wise sayings that have been handed down through time and culture that suggest how you should live.

Honesty is the best policy. People in glass houses shouldn't throw stones. Don't throw good money after bad. The early bird gets the worm. Well done is better than well said.

You've heard these sayings.

They clearly carry some kind of practical power, because people simply abide by them without even caring who the original author was. I've met many people like that married couple who have successful long-term relationships and lives despite not following Christ. They've simply applied the wisdom that works, putting it into action in their lives.

But how much better would it be to know the author and have a relationship with the one whose words you are living by? To just enjoy the benefits without acknowledging the author is like a toddler excitedly ripping off the wrapping paper on the Christmas presents without caring whose name is on the tag.

What do we as adults tell them? "Honey, say thank you to uncle so and so …"

You've probably heard "go the extra mile" or "turn the other cheek" said by someone, maybe even our politicians in an election year! It's more good wisdom, more great aphorisms. The difference is, we know who said it: Jesus Christ.

What does "go the extra mile" mean? It's when you go above and beyond what is expected.

In Matthew 5, Jesus said, "And if anyone forces you to go one mile, go with him two miles." In Jesus's day, Roman soldiers who occupied Israel were harsh and could force them to do things without question. However, the soldiers weren't allowed to demand that someone carry their luggage or belongings more than one mile.

Jesus is telling people to do more than what is expected.

Jesus carries this idea out further, telling people to "turn the other cheek" when you've been slapped, or to give someone your outer garment if they've sued you for your inner garment.

Doing more than is expected of you is great wisdom. It will help with your relationships with others and create in you a right attitude while also giving you the opportunity to practice humility and hard work.

Yet while taking action and doing the work to live by wisdom is great, it's even better to graduate from doing something just because it works to doing something because you're in a relationship with the author. Whoever has your hope has your heart. Is your hope in the wise words, or the author of those words?

CHANGING YOUR TRAJECTORY

When I was 50 years old, people would ask me what I thought I'd be doing in the next ten years. I told them that while I didn't know exactly what I was going to do, I knew what I would *not* be doing anymore. I wouldn't fight foolish fights. I wouldn't give my life and energy to the wind or to vain pursuits.

> **SOME OF US WILL HAVE CHASED AFTER FOOLISH THINGS AND HAVE HAD MULTIPLE WRECKS IN LIFE. BUT EVEN IN THE MIDST OF CONSEQUENCES, THERE'S A LIGHT OF HOPE.**

Book titles today easily lure us into chasing vain pursuits. Get a bigger business, better body, try these life hacks, make your life go better right now—if you want it, someone will promise it.

Simply chasing after what you want from day to day is fickle and foolish. It's wisdom to know what you no longer want. This doesn't mean we live our lives looking backwards. It means realizing that your past alone does not define you, but instead becomes a reference point for your future course.

So, let's pivot. Knowing what you don't want anymore is just as important as knowing what you do want.

John came into my office burdened, even though he heard wisdom every Sunday. It made me wonder how many people repeat their 20-year-old mistakes at 50.

At life's end, we clearly see our should-haves and shouldn't-haves.

Some of us will have chased after foolish things and have had multiple wrecks in life. But even in the midst of consequences, there's a light of hope.

There's the opportunity to ask the Holy Spirit to help us change our thinking, to start a new trajectory towards wisdom and stability. God is in the business of trading beauty for ashes and making all things new.

In Proverbs we see three categories of people when it comes to dealing with wisdom. The wise, the foolish, and the simple. The wise person embraces wisdom like a lifeline. The foolish person turns their back and spurns her offer of insight and prudence. The simple person is undecided, maybe just drifting along and letting old patterns and everyday circumstances decide.

Who do you want to be?

If you'd rather walk in wisdom, then continue reading. Proverbs tells us how to get started.

CHAPTER ONE REFLECTIONS:
HOW'S IT GOING SO FAR?

1) We just described three characters found in Proverbs: the wise, the foolish and the simple. What kind of life choices might each one be making that would land them in one of those categories? Have you ever found yourself going with or against "the grain of life," and how did that work out for you? What did the fruit of each category look like?

2) If your house was on fire, what would you try to rescue from the flames and why? If this suddenly was the last week of your life, what would you say were the most valuable things to you? Where would your steps go? Who would you want to speak with and what would the conversation be about?

3) As each year passes by, do your value judgments change? In what ways and why do you think that is?

CHAPTER TWO

You Have to Choose a Side

"The remarkable thing about God is that when you fear God, you fear nothing else, whereas if you do not fear God, you fear everything else."
– Oswald Chambers

"Through love and faithfulness sin is atoned for; through the fear of the Lord evil is avoided."
– Proverbs 16:6 (NIV)

"Who among the gods is like you, Lord? Who is like you—majestic in holiness, awesome in glory, working wonders?"
– Exodus 15:11 (NIV)

All Dash wanted to do was win the race. And he was easily the fastest kid on the track, faster than probably every other child on the planet and an uncommonly good runner.

But Dash wasn't allowed to embrace the uncommon.

In the 2004 Pixar movie *The Incredibles*, a family of superheroes with amazing powers are struggling to fit into regular society. Dash, the young son, is able to run fast and could easily win all races if only his parents would let him. When he ran, he was a blur, at the starting line one moment and at the finish in the next.

But that kind of speed would draw attention to him and his family. While arguing with his mom about being allowed to use his full potential, he tells her that "our powers make us special."

"Everyone is special, Dash," she replies.

"Which is another way of saying no one is," he says, slumping back into the cushion of the car seat.

There's a lot being said in that little scene, but it's a poignant commentary on the downside to our culture's pursuit of equality and justice. With a noble goal of making certain that no one is favored unfairly, we inadvertently flattened the structures to make it so no one is above anyone else. We've created a culture where rising above and thinking someone is above us isn't allowed.

In a flat landscape, nothing stands out, nothing towers above.

And so we end up with two extremes. At one end, we honor people based on their performance and fame; and in that way, we become a works-based, performance-driven culture where we might not rise above, but we could get ahead. At the other extreme, no one is worthy of honor.

God tells us He is holy.

The opposite of holy is not just seeing something as being worldly or sinful. Rather, it's taking something wonderful, beautiful, and unique and making it altogether common. Throughout the Old Testament, the idols that God's people fashioned and bowed down to looked suspiciously like their makers (Isaiah 44).

God has given each of us our own unique gift. It's something that makes us distinctive and exceptional, one of a kind. Our enemy knows that if he can pollute that gift, if he can contaminate it and make it common, he can immobilize you. The call or gifting that God once placed on your life becomes a distant memory, and what was unique about you gets replaced by the status quo.

Whether it's sexuality, worship, marriage, identity, character—whatever it is, the danger lies in making what God intended to be holy and sacred into some kind of cheap commodity that can be changed or exchanged when we feel like it.

A good example of that is the difference between simply having sex and having sexual intimacy. Worship, to a life with Christ, is what sexuality is to a marriage. It's an expression of intimacy and a declaration of faithfulness. No small wonder so much focus is on promiscuity and sexual permissiveness in today's culture because what our culture has made out to be something you do with your body for pleasure actually chips away at the foundational metaphor for life in Christ.

During a wedding ceremony, I point out that the purpose of the ring is to illustrate a closed circle. Before a couple is married, they could go with someone else. But in front of all the people witnessing the ceremony, they are letting the world know they're closing the circle. No one gets in except the two being married. There's an exclusion at work, something rare and even mysterious, something exclusive.

They are entering into a holy place.

GOD IS HOLY

When God says, "I am holy," He's not bragging. He's telling us He is altogether different than anything we know.

He's not being some unreasonable authority figure or a big egotist. When God says He is holy, He's making a statement of fact. He's the only one who can make that claim, and He wants us to hear Him.

> GOD BEING HOLY MEANS THAT HE IS IN CHARGE OF IT ALL, DOWN TO THE LAST MOLECULE. HE'S FLYING THE PLANE, AND HIS INSTRUCTIONS ARE THE ONES WE SHOULD LISTEN TO CAREFULLY.

Think of it like this: if I'm boarding the airplane to fly to Dallas, whose opinion should I listen to when it comes to how to properly behave on the airplane? The man sitting next to me? The opinion of the woman across the aisle? I want to listen to the pilot flying the plane when he gives instructions for the passengers. Why? Because he really is different from the rest of us passengers in one very important aspect: he's the one flying the plane.

God being holy means that He is in charge of it all, down to the last molecule. He's flying the plane, and His instructions are the ones we should listen to carefully. In the book of Job, we see both Job and his friends trying to figure out what God is doing in a world gone terribly wrong. After 37 chapters of their lectures to each other, God shows up in a whirlwind and gives them an eye-opening pop quiz beginning with the words, *"Who is this that questions my wisdom with such ignorant words? Brace yourself like a man, because I have some questions for you, and you must answer them. Where were you when I laid the foundations of the earth? Tell me, if you know so much"* (Job 38:2–4 NLT).

Job's response to God at the end of it all is, *"I had only heard about you before, but now I have seen you with my own eyes. I take back everything I said, and I sit in dust and ashes to show my repentance"* (Job 42:5–6). Don't miss Job's heart response. I sit and I repent. I am the one who needs to change, not God. That's one example of what the fear of the Lord looks like. I stop talking and arguing and posturing, and I listen. I listen to the opinion that matters the most. I listen to wisdom that comes from outside of myself.

However, if my heart is cynical, jaded, or rebellious, that's very hard to accept. Who is God to tell me what to do?! Who is He to say He is the most high?! Both the Scripture and human history are littered with stories of peoples and ideologies that have taken their stand against God in that way. It always ends poorly because who are we to ignore a holy God?

What good is reverence for a holy God? How could something that seems so big and vague and outside of daily life have any impact right now? One of the most staggering promises of God made to a backslidden priest in the Old Testament was "He who honors me I will honor"

(1 Samuel 2:30). Stop for a moment and reflect on the implications of God's offer there.

English playwright Dorothy Sayers said that God endured three humiliations for us. The first was in a stable where Jesus was born, surrendering His heavenly home to become a human. The second was at the cross where Jesus was falsely accused, mocked, beaten, and executed. The third is the church itself, as God allows us to represent His Son, Jesus, here on earth. A God who rarely steps in to defend Himself when we embarrass Him! If I owned the company, I would have a few words with those who were misrepresenting my good graces to a watching world. But the head remains patiently silent while the body slowly works out her salvation day by day.

A holy God deserves none of that, but God did it anyway to save us. The Designer and the Creator wants to be a part of your everyday life.

LIVING IN GOD'S ECONOMY

There are times when I've had the opportunity to meet with a couple about to be married who are not believers in Christ. Like any couple, they are seeking advice on how to have a marriage that will be fulfilling and enjoyable. During our conversation about how they are going to join their lives together, I often draw a diagram using three vertical boxes that line up over the top of each other.

Pointing to the top box, I tell them that this is who God claims to be. You don't have to believe it; but God claims to be the Designer, the Origin, and the Idea behind the universe. There was a creative and wise intelligence that made everything, and God claims to be that Architect.

Pointing to the second box, I tell them that God doesn't only claim to be the Designer but also the Creator. He didn't just think of how everything should be, but He actually brought His design to life by His power. Usually, for the first two boxes, even the unbelievers are in some form of agreement. It is often "the man upstairs" kind of idea that we hear so often. But then the third box comes into the picture.

"God also claims to be the 'maintenance guy,'" I say, pointing to the bottom box. "He claims to be the Maintainer of the entire universe, keeping everything running and in order, including you and me."

It's as if the architect who designed the 50-story condo then became the contractor for the same project and then chose to move into his own creation. And that's where it gets uncomfortable for most people. We can accept there's a "big guy upstairs" who designed and created, but we don't want him living next door to us and messing with our daily lives.

Remember John, who came to my office, struggling to make a life that worked? He lived his own life Monday through Saturday, only giving God Sunday. His daily life didn't correspond to having a fear of God. He didn't want God living with him there every day. He forgot about Emmanuel ("God with us") and preferred a God at a distance, one who was on call when he needed Him.

That's a big problem.

God holds all things together (Colossians 1:17). It's an active state. And that means He wants to be speaking to you about your social life, your work life, and your family life. He wants to keep you from evil; He wants you to avoid wandering into temptation; He wants to help guard you from money and greed destroying your life. He wants you to have a life that is lived well and that flourishes in every way. This not only blesses us but also blesses others; and in so doing, it reflects that goodness of God to a watching world. Proverbs tells us the fear of the Lord is the beginning of wisdom, so we have to deal with that fact. We have to take it up with the Maintenance Director, but that's hard to do if we've pushed Him out of the building.

It's the day-to-day part of the equation that often causes the problem that keeps people from going to church and never moving beyond nodding to the Guy Upstairs and living life as they want. We prefer the idea that God is watching from a distance, letting us live our lives as we see fit.

We say we can be whatever we want. But God says otherwise. He has designed the world and how everything in it works, including our appetites and desires. We've "fixed" this inconvenient truth by making God in our own image, telling ourselves He's like us. "God is love!" we say as the justification for a lot of sin, not bothering to define what the love of a holy God actually looks like.

We create structures or systems to function how we want them to, pretending we're not bound by God's economy, and then wondering why things are going badly.

We all live in God's economy—which is very different from the culture in this world. Jesus is King, whether I voted for Him or not. Not everyone believes that about God, but God Himself makes that claim. He tells us He is holy, righteous, and good; and there is no one like Him. He created all things and knows the way things work best.

And in God's universe, there is value placed on who and what we honor, not just performance or achievement.

GOD BLESSES THOSE WHO SHOW HONOR

Honor is tied both to performance and position. Specifically in American culture, we often honor those who have accumulated fame, money, or power. In God's eyes, things work differently, both in who we honor and in the outcome of that honor.

For example, when God tells us to honor our parents, there's a promise given back to us: our life will be better because of it (Exodus 20:12). Even when we have had parents who have acted dishonorably towards us, the choice is still ours. I can treat them with contempt or honor them if for nothing else but because of their position. They gave me life, and maybe that's all I can find to recognize them for; but I now have the opportunity to live this life well. I am in charge of my response, and I choose to be a person of honor regardless of what others have done. I refuse to respond to dishonor with dishonor.

After Noah left the ark, he planted a vineyard and, unfortunately, got drunk and passed out with the wine his own vines had produced. His youngest son, Ham, saw his father lying naked in the tent and proceeded to broadcast the news to his brothers, Shem and Japeth.

"Hey you guys! Dad's drunk and naked!" you can almost hear Ham saying, shaking his head with a chuckle. But Shem and Japeth refused to dishonor their father and look upon his shame. So, draping a cloth over their shoulders, they backed in and covered him. When Noah woke up, he cursed Ham for his contemptuous behavior.

That wasn't a one-off moment in the Bible. It's a consistent idea throughout. Proverbs 14:26 says that whoever fears God has a secure fortress; and for their children, it will be a refuge. That's a promise not only to us now but also one that impacts the next generation. Instead of sending chaos and dysfunction forward, fearing a holy God now creates a refuge for you and your children.

But if you don't fear God, you don't live in that place of protection. You live with a back door open, allowing anyone— and any lie—to come into your life. You're susceptible to the fear of man because there's no strong fortress around you, and you send that down to your children.

WHEN FEAR IS GOOD

My grandson and I were talking one night before bedtime.

"Papa," he asked. "Does God know everything?"

"Well … yes. I believe He does."

"You mean, like everything in our past *and* our future?" That's deep theology for an 8-year-old.

"Yes, He sees all our past and He knows what our future holds," I said. "He tells us in Psalms that He knows the number of days that are written in our book. That He knew us before we were born, and He knows when we'll die. So yes, I believe He knows everything."

"That's amazing." My grandson was quiet for a moment. "But don't you think that's kind of creepy?"

I laughed. In a way, it was frightening. That's part of the healthy fear of the Lord. God is so far beyond us it should move us to awe and wonder. But now, think of the counterfeit. There's a young man, eighteen years old, still living under his parent's roof. He takes his girlfriend out on a date, and then they go park by the ocean to watch the sunset. Pretty soon, the hormones kick in, and they're both well on the way to an intimacy they feel is beyond their control.

The train has left the station.

But suddenly the young man's little brother pops up in the back seat. He's been hiding back there, to the surprise of those in the front seat.

"Hey, what are you guys doing?"

There's a mad rush, and they come to a stop. It is all over. The train comes to a screeching halt.

When I tell this story to youth groups, my next question is, "what do you really believe about God?"

Do you think He is everywhere, seeing everything including the good and the evil? Because if you do, that means you'd not only stop for your little brother but you'd also stop for God's sake. You're embarrassed in front of your little brother, afraid he's going to rat you out; but you're not embarrassed in the presence of the all-powerful God.

"I couldn't help myself," I'll often hear. "I was caught up. The heart wants what the heart wants."

In other words, they are at the mercy of their emotions. But are we really that helpless?

Imagine a single guy who goes alone to a wedding. He's at the reception table with champagne and food; and he helps himself, filling a plate and pouring a glass. Suddenly, a beautiful woman walks up and asks him if he'd pour her a glass of that champagne.

Just like that, his antenna goes up and he's interested.

"What's your name? Where are you from?" he asks, chatting her up. He's already gone to a place in his heart where he's imagining that perhaps he has finally found the one he has been waiting for. She's not flirting, only asking for a glass; but he has other ideas. The emotions are there, the words are there, the ideas are there, the potential seems to be there … and then another guy walks up.

"This is my husband, Tom," the woman says. Turning to her husband, she introduces him to the single guy.

And just like that, everything is turned off.

The power to control ourselves, to get our emotions and desires into check, is there. Using emotions and a lack of self-control as an excuse for disobedience to God is simply preferring to indulge or disobey. We don't value God's holiness enough to obey Him.

The little brother you didn't realize was in the backseat, the husband you didn't know about—they'll get you to stop. But the presence of a holy God won't? You don't fear God enough that it would change how you live in His constant presence?

God is worthy, He is holy, and He is King of kings and Lord of lords above everything else. But if you don't live with a genuine reverence of this reality, you won't see Him that way. You will live as if God is underwhelming, unimpressive, and without weight in our everyday lives. David Wells describes it like this: "It is one of the defining marks of Our Time that God is now weightless. I do not mean by this that he is ethereal, but rather that he has become unimportant. He rests upon the world so inconsequentially as not to be noticeable ..." The "fear of the Lord" is mentioned over 150 times in God's Word, and many of those are found in Proverbs. If something is mentioned 150 times, it might do us good to investigate it. So, why does this get so little attention? In all your years sitting in church, how many messages have you heard on the fear of the Lord? Not that many, perhaps because we instinctively think all fear is harmful or limiting?

This isn't your typical fear, though.

The fear of the Lord isn't some morbid, paralyzing fear. It's a fear that protects me, building understanding that there is something bigger than me.

> GOD IS WORTHY, HE IS HOLY, AND HE IS KING OF KINGS AND LORD OF LORDS ABOVE EVERYTHING ELSE. BUT IF YOU DON'T LIVE WITH A GENUINE REVERENCE OF THIS REALITY, YOU WON'T SEE HIM THAT WAY.

A healthy fear keeps us from dangling off the railing at the Grand Canyon, with thousands of feet of nothing below. A healthy fear keeps us from grabbing the hot electrical wire. We don't walk around morbidly afraid to visit the Grand Canyon or flip on the light switch; instead, our fear keeps us safe and helps us understand the limitations around us. Instead of being roadblocks, His commands now become the guardrails that allow me to fully enjoy everything good and beautiful He has placed in my life—without going over the cliff.

When it comes to God, it's critically important to understand our limitations. We're human. God is divine. And we need to honor that divinity, which translates into a daily life of walking in humility. It means a life of not leaning on our own understanding, but acknowledging God's ways instead (Proverbs 3:5–6). In return, He promises that living a life in healthy reverence of Him will be a constant source of healing to us.

Unfortunately, many people rely on external motivations to guide their behavior. In the church world, using hell as a threat or heaven as a bribe has never produced healthy relationships with the Father of our souls.

Neither one has anything to do with fearing a holy God in a way that leads to faith, trust, and love. It's not enough to just say "yeah, God is big and powerful!" and hope He doesn't strike you with lightning if you say a bad word.

True fear of God is a reverence that creates an attitude in us that acknowledges how powerful and amazing God is, a reverence that leads to a life that aligns with a holy God.

Reverential fear of God is the cornerstone of trust, and it's also the foundation of truly good character.

CHARACTER AND INTEGRITY

When I was in middle school, they were building several new houses at the end of the street in our development. The houses were framed, but not much else was done.

Sitting with my friends on the front porch one Saturday morning, we got the idea to go and play in those barely framed houses. They looked much more exciting than any playground. We started down the street just as my dad walked by and headed to his car.

"Where are you guys going?"

We told him we were going to play in the housing project.

"Absolutely not. You can't do that," he said. He pointed out that it wasn't our property. Then he told us it wasn't safe. He gave more of the usual warnings parents give kids who were about to do something stupid. Then he walked away.

I was so embarrassed. My dad seemed like such a killjoy in front of my friends.

"We're going down there anyway," my friends said, making a point of telling me that my dad wasn't their dad. They took off, and I sat there alone on the front porch. After a while, I decided to go down to the houses. What could go wrong? What did my dad know anyway? I trotted down the street and found my friends having a great time in the framed houses.

There we were running through the houses, which were bi-level and gave us the opportunity to jump from the living room down to the floor below. At one point, I jumped down onto what I thought was the floor; but it was a thin piece of plywood that covered up a stairwell. I went right through that wood and fell all the way down to the basement, cracking my head open and landing on a pile of rocks. Blood was pouring out of my head, and I was sure I was dying.

Somehow I managed to get out and run towards home, blood flowing from my head and splattering the sidewalk. My shirt was soaked in blood, and I was sure my brains were coming out. About the time I arrived home, Dad pulled up in the driveway. He stepped out of his car and looked at me, a bloody mess and in a panic. I will never forget his words—a question instead of a scolding.

"Why didn't you trust me?" he said.

I expected punishment, but all dad would say was, "why didn't you trust me?"

So, why didn't I trust my dad? At the time, I thought Dad was stealing my joy. I hated discipline and correction. It felt like an unnecessary restriction. It was Proverbs 12:13–14 lived out. My dad knew what dangers were there. He knew what partial construction was like. We didn't.

Not only did I not trust my dad's advice, but I didn't honor him enough to stay back on that front porch instead of running after my friends. Obedience to God requires faith, and that requires trust. Hebrews 11 is called the faith chapter of the Bible, and it is full of people who trust and obey God despite not knowing, not seeing, and not understanding.

What led all those saints to trust in God? Why do we trust?

Because of character. Who He really is and who we really are matters. Often when I read a book on leadership, the author will mention that good character is vitally important. But they leave it there, as if there were many ways to have good character and you just need to find what works for you.

Imagine you're in a restaurant, and the service has been terrible. When the bill arrives, you have a choice to make. Will you refuse to tip because the service was poor? Or will you tip because being generous is a part of who you are, regardless of someone else's actions?

Your character is determined by the foundation you've built your life on. It's shaped by your day-to-day decisions that add up to become your day-to-day life. Little actions become habits that, whether good or bad, will ultimately become a lifestyle. When I develop the practice of getting to know the character of the One who calls me to trust Him, I find it far easier to obey Him. As I develop the practice of yielding to Him, I find that my life becomes predictable and dependable to some degree.

In fact, show me a person who walks humbly in a daily awareness of God's presence, and I can pretty much predict how they will respond in moments of testing or temptation, regardless of who is around. That's what integrity looks like. I no longer depend on the external forces of the law to keep me in line. I am now living from the inside out. I think this is what the Psalmist meant when he said, "He leads me in paths of righteousness for His name's sake." Life with all its pressures always seeks to drive me to do or to be, while our Father wants to lead me into what is good. Is my life rooted in a reverence for the good and infinitely wise God, or am I simply living according to my own rules?

I should have trusted my dad because of his wisdom and character, knowing he didn't want me to be harmed. I chose my own way and suffered because of it. Suffering for a good cause is a noble thing, but suffering for my own foolishness is a bitter medicine.

Who we trust and why we trust them has an impact on our own character. In his book *The Nature and Character of God*, the author Winkie Pratney puts it this way: "God's right to govern is based on His qualifications, the implementation of that right is based on His ability. The revelation of His character is the basis of our glad surrender to Him." This helps explain both the mystery and the attraction of a life of faith in God. I will never completely understand His mind or His ways; but based on what He has revealed about Himself, I see consistency that convinces me He is trustworthy.

WHAT ARE YOU HUNGRY FOR?

What are you actually hungry for?

If you're reading this book, my guess is that you're hungry for a life that works, that is effective and enjoyable in the long run. But what does that actually look like? It's not just an idea hanging out there in thin air; it's built on character and integrity in your everyday life. That means you can't live life Monday through Saturday on your rules and leave Sunday for God. The problems happen Monday through Saturday, too.

Just as an athlete or performer excels at their sport not just through natural ability but because of consistent practice, we must practice wisdom by living in reverential fear of the holy God.

Do you really want to be wise? Are you sincere about seeking truth? Seeking seems to describe a lot of people these days. It's kind of "in style." True seekers, however, have arrived at a point in their lives where they are genuinely open to truth whatever the cost. They are always willing to let go of one thing to reach for what they believe to be the better thing. This is a lifelong process of maturing. Os Guinness says in *The Journey*: "The point is not that people believe in God because of need, that would be irrational and make the believer vulnerable to the accusation that faith is a crutch. Rather they disbelieve in what they believed in before because of new needs that their previous beliefs could not answer." We come to the end of ourselves and admit we're ready to lay down our ideas and listen. Disbelief is a good beginning, but don't stop there.

"I thought the answer was self-indulgence, but it's not."

"I thought the answer was self-rule, but it's not."

"I thought the answer was self-exaltation, but it's not."

This discovery was witnessed in the writings of St. Augustine who arrived at this conclusion in his journey for truth: "You have made us for yourself, O Lord, and **our heart** is **restless** until it rests in you."

In the end, we all must serve somebody. Paul declared in Romans that we are either a slave to sin or a slave to righteousness, but he didn't leave room for any other position (Romans 6). Phillips Brooks, the Episcopal clergyman and writer, said: "No man in this world attains to freedom from any slavery except by entering into some higher form of servitude. There is no such thing as an entirely free man."

Joshua clearly drew the line with God's people early on in their history with him as they journeyed towards their promised land. "And if it is evil in your eyes to serve the LORD, choose this day whom you will serve, whether the gods your fathers served in the region beyond the River, or the gods of the Amorites in whose land you dwell. But as for me and my house, we will serve the LORD" (Joshua 24:15). The gods of the land are a trap. The fear of man, Proverbs says, is a snare. That Hebrew word *snare* is used to provoke an image of having a hook in our nose, but whoever trusts in God is kept safe (Proverbs 29:25). If you can put a hook in someone's nose, no matter how big and powerful they are, no matter their gifts, no matter what God intended for them … you can lead them anywhere.

> WHAT IF REAL FREEDOM IS NOT THE POWER TO DO WHATEVER WE PLEASE WHEN WE PLEASE, BUT THE POWER TO BECOME ALL THAT WE WERE DESIGNED BY OUR CREATOR TO BE?

In our hearts, we long for freedom. What if real freedom is not the power to do whatever we please when we please, but the power to become all that we were designed by our Creator to be?

CHAPTER TWO REFLECTIONS:
NAVIGATING DESIRES, FEARS, AND DIVINE TRUST

1) Can you look back at a time when you indulged in something that promised you some measure of fulfillment, but it failed to deliver and left you diminished instead of enriched? Where was your heavenly Father then? Were you asking His opinion? Was it hard to hear His voice and heart and if so, why? What was missing?

2) What kind of fears play into the everyday decisions you make? What do those voices sound like and how do they seek to influence you? Are there areas where certain fears seem to carry more weight and, in turn, cause you more grief?

3) In looking at the character of God, what do you see in Him that should give you confidence to trust Him even if you don't understand it at the moment? Make a list of five things that God says about Himself that help you yield to His care in your life.

CHAPTER THREE

Whatever Else You Get

"Insanity is doing the same thing over and over again and expecting different results."
– Author Unknown

"When I was a boy at my father's knee, the pride and joy of my mother, He would sit me down and drill me:"Take this to heart. Do what I tell you—live! Sell everything and buy Wisdom! Forage for Understanding! Don't forget one word! Don't deviate an inch! Never walk away from Wisdom—she guards your life; love her— she keeps her eye on you. Above all, do this: Get Wisdom! Write this at the top of your list: Get Understanding! Throw your arms around her—believe me, you won't regret it; never let her go—she'll make your life glorious. She'll garland your life with grace, she'll festoon your days with beauty."
– Proverbs 4:3–9 (MSG)

Every weekday, for decades, a man spent hours in traffic—
blaring horns, the smell of exhaust, watching his car burn
through pricey fuel while going nowhere. Even though the
bumper-to-bumper traffic was frustrating, he found it gave him
lots of time to daydream.

He pictured the perfect cabin hidden in the mountains.
He could see how it would look inside and out. As the years
went on, his dream became more detailed. He knew exactly
how his cabin would be built. He knew exactly where he wanted
it to be. He knew the location almost better than any place he
currently visited because he spent so much time dreaming of it.

Snow-peaked mountains rising high all around, draped
with deep green spruce and patches of aspen trees. Sharp rocks
mixed with softer tumbling rock falls, poking up through the
foliage. In the fall, those aspens would turn gold, whispering
in the crisp breezes, sunlight bouncing off the round leaves
like golden beams of light shooting in every direction. A gentle
sloping green valley divided by a crystal-clear mountain river
would be at the heart of it. And that's where his dream cabin
would be, right by the river bend. Clean air, clean water, only
the sound of nature, and no more traffic.

The day arrived when his dream came true.

He found that cabin. He bought that cabin. And he set
about making his new life there. There were no noisy neighbors,
no sounds of lawnmowers or barking dogs or honking horns.
Each morning was a fresh sunrise and a chance to do a little
fishing or sip a cup of coffee down at the edge of the river,
watching the trout dart around the rocks in the clear water.

One morning, sitting in his favorite spot with his mug of coffee and fishing equipment nearby, he saw something in the water. Where the rocks had formed an eddy, he could see trash bobbing, trapped in the circular current.

Immediately, he felt a sense of rage. What was this polluting trash doing in his perfect valley?

He got a shovel and his fishing rod, and he began pulling the garbage out of the water and putting it into a bucket. He managed to clear the trash, and seeing his full bucket brought him a sense of accomplishment.

A few days later, more garbage floated in the water. This time he watched as it floated downstream, bobbing along until it was caught up in the eddy. There seemed to be a bit more, bouncing around, mocking him, dropping bits of filth into that perfectly clear water. Again, he fished it out.

The third time it happened, he realized he needed a better approach. He couldn't spend every day dreading the arrival of the trash. He didn't want to keep getting angry as he fished it out.

I have to go upstream and see where this is coming from, he thought as he set down his bucket and shovel. His wonderful life along the mountain river wasn't supposed to be lived as a trash collector. Setting off on foot, hiking along the rivers' edge, he was determined to put an end to the source of the garbage once and for all.

We can be a lot like that man. We work hard to live a life that works, and it can seem as if all our hard work and striving are making it happen. But for some reason, garbage starts piling up in our lives; and we spend a lot of time and energy on trash removal instead of a more effective approach to things.

A more satisfying solution might be investigating and dealing with the source—the issues causing all the grief. Because no matter how many times you clear out the trash popping up in your life, it will keep coming back until you find out what's going on upstream.

WHY DO YOU DO WHAT YOU DO?

Do you ever stop to consider why you do what you do? What's your motivation? What lens do you view your life through? Where did your habits come from?

These are important questions to ask. Our internal definition of success comes from the lens we observe life through, the lens that informs our decisions. Use the wrong lens, and you'll have the wrong motivation, the wrong engine driving your every thought and action.

Everything we do is motivated by something internal, though many of us don't take the time to dig deep to discover what that is. In my years of working with people, I've come to think that there are three basic motivations that people work from.

It's All About Me

The first motivation is the baseline, where we do what we do for ourselves. This is easy to see in a toddler's life. We expect this of them because, at this stage and from their perspective, the world does sort of revolve around them! Toddlers can be adorable even if they are self-centered.

This sounds like an automatically negative thing, but it's not always as bad as it sounds. We go to work to get paid. We work to get money to buy food and pay our rent. We do these things to look after ourselves and our family. From that aspect, it makes sense.

But at some point, that motivation alone can become very self-centered or, at the very least, immature.

As a long-term missionary, I watched people come on mission trips to help in orphanages. We didn't have to work as hard to convince them to come serve overseas and help with missions when an orphanage was involved. That's a great thing, of course. We want people to care and serve.

But the fact is that some returned repeatedly to be able to hold the babies and get that immediate emotional rush from doing an overtly good thing. They *are* doing a good thing; and while it's not wrong to want to do that, at the very baseline, they could still be doing it for themselves and how it makes them feel. They might even be doing it to let others know how good they are, so they feel even better. Virtue signaling in our day has become a not-so-subtle art form.

Operating on this baseline carries the danger of using people and situations for what we get out of them. When our motivation operates from this baseline, if we don't get what we want or if life doesn't go our way, we're going to be hard to live with. We have all observed what happens when that cute little toddler doesn't get their way. They let people around them know they are not happy. We'll break off relationships if the other person isn't giving us what we want. We'll quit serving in organizations. We'll stop donating. We want what we want, and that's what's driving us.

It's All About Helping Others

The second motivation is that we do things because we want to help others.

This sounds like the best motivation, doesn't it? Helping others is how we change the world, we're told. Someone motivated to help others could be an activist or a missionary, a member of the Peace Corps, or a volunteer in a homeless ministry—if some worthy cause is out there, that's where you'll find them.

Helping others seems very Biblical, and it's certainly a step above the previous level. But there's a catch, and it has to do with the heart. This is still a vulnerable position because our emotional well-being still often depends on others. We want to help others, and with that comes a need to know we have helped them. We're easily disappointed if gratefulness or acknowledgement aren't returned. We expect someone somewhere to recognize that we have helped. We want to see some kind of measurable results from our service because those results affirm us and make us feel good.

The temptation to quit runs high if helping others is your sole motivation. You genuinely want to help, but you certainly expect those getting the help to express thankfulness. At some point, the returned thankfulness won't be quite enough, or your work won't be recognized. You'll feel very empty and burned out and wonder if your sacrifice was actually useful. This is particularly true for people who work in very difficult places where human brokenness and injustice runs deep throughout the culture and gratitude is nowhere to be found. What can help me to remain faithful to my calling with some measure of joy in my heart?

Is He Worthy?

The third motivation is entirely different than the previous two.

In 2 Timothy chapter 4, Paul writes from prison how different friends and ministry partners have abandoned or betrayed him. "At my first defense, no one came to my support," he wrote. "Everyone deserted me. May it not be held against them." That sounds like a discouraging scenario. Unjustly imprisoned and then abandoned by his companions sound like a recipe for a pity party.

But here's where we see Paul's motivation revealed. "But the Lord stood by me and gave me strength, so that through me the message might be fully proclaimed and all the gentiles might hear it" (2 Tim. 4:17). "I have fought the good fight; I have finished the race; I have kept the faith" (2 Tim. 4:7).

Paul would have never made it through all he experienced if he was only looking out for himself or just wanted to help people. His letters would have been full of complaints if he had—much like we see on social media—because he was certainly seeing no return for all his efforts.

No, his motivation was something very different. His motivation was simply because Jesus was worthy. He viewed every experience in life through the lens of knowing that Jesus was worth every sacrifice regardless of how people responded to him.

What if we do what we do because Jesus is worthy? When that's the motivation for how we operate, we can become untouchable by people or circumstances. It doesn't matter if someone deserts us or thanks us or makes us feel good about ourselves or abandons us. Jesus will always be worthy, and the center of our motivation holds.

It's a motivation that doesn't make sense by the standards of worldly wisdom. The world says that success is measured in numbers. This dangerous practice can be found inside and outside the church. In church, we calculate success in life by nickels and noses; and outside church, it's by square footage and followers. We make good deeds public to gather likes because, if no one knows it happened, how can we get any credit for it?

Can you imagine the good that could be accomplished in our world if we no longer cared who got the credit for it? A missionary dedicates his life to a foreign field and sees only one convert. A translator spends a lifetime translating the Bible into an obscure language and dies before seeing any return. Someone serves the poor and needy without any worldly acclaim. Someone gives their resources and only cares that God sees. This kind of perseverance is only possible when Jesus is seen as worthy. Viewed through the lens of temporal measurements, this kind of living will always be seen as an oddity or even a waste.

At the end of his life, Jesus wasn't successful by the world's standards. He'd thinned out disciples, was deserted by most of his followers, never built a temple, never wrote a book, and never built personal wealth. Yet in God's economy, Jesus's life was a success, expressed by, "I have brought you glory on the earth by finishing the work that you gave me to do" (John 17:4).

What motivates you? What value defines how you operate? Are you functioning in the world's economy or God's?

When we operate our daily life on the idea that we do what we do because Jesus is worthy, disappointment and tragedy don't slow us down for long. The storms don't stop us. We don't quit. We don't give up. We have nothing to lose and everything to gain.

~

WHEN WE OPERATE OUR DAILY LIFE ON THE IDEA THAT WE DO WHAT WE DO BECAUSE JESUS IS WORTHY, DISAPPOINTMENT AND TRAGEDY DON'T SLOW US DOWN FOR LONG. THE STORMS DON'T STOP US. WE DON'T QUIT. WE DON'T GIVE UP. WE HAVE NOTHING TO LOSE AND EVERYTHING TO GAIN.

~

THREE WAYS OF GAINING WISDOM

Chinese philosopher Confucius said that there were three ways to gain wisdom. The first is reflection, which is the highest. The second is the easiest: imitation. The third is experience, which is the most bitter.

In other words, you can gain wisdom through study, self-restriction, and experience. Let's take a deeper look at those three approaches to gaining wisdom by imagining that we're in a kitchen with a hot stove top that our friend, Debbie, has just placed her hand on. As a result, she is now dealing with an ugly burn.

Gaining Wisdom Through Reflection

"I've studied hot stoves. I know how human skin reacts to heat. My teachers have taught me the physics involved. I'm not going to touch the stove."

This method allows you to acquire wisdom by trusting a teacher and the results of study.

Gaining Wisdom Through Observation

You can gain wisdom by observing what happens to someone else. This is the idea of self-restriction or limitation.

"Wow, Debbie just put her hand on the hot stove and got a serious burn! I'm never going to touch a hot stove."

In this way, you observe and acquire wisdom at the expense of another person's experience.

Gaining Wisdom Through Experience

You can also gain wisdom by experiencing something yourself.

"Even though Debbie got burned, I'm special. That won't happen to me. I can touch the stove and it'll be okay."

In this way, you acquire wisdom painfully and have to live with consequences along with that new understanding. This method rejects godly wisdom in favor of finding out for yourself, trying to forge your own path without listening to a guide. Our fathers would have called this *learning the hard way*. I have heard people describe this learning style as something to be proud of, but I am not sure this is a pattern I want to live my life by. We are all going to use at least one of these three methods as we go through life. But it is the last one, rejecting God's wisdom in favor of finding your own way, that leads to pain without some redeeming value. The writer of Proverbs describes it over and over as foolishness. He tells us that, "The way of fools seems right to them, but the wise listen to advice" (Proverbs 12:15).

SORTING THROUGH THE MESS

On a morning flight to Denver from Portland, I talked to the man next to me. Over coffee, I took the time to get to know him. He worked as a research chemist in the oil industry of Colorado, and he was heading home.

He was very intelligent and shared with me all kinds of information about the work he did. As he was telling me about the soil, about oil, and the Earth being billions of years old, I realized I probably wasn't talking to a believer. But I was enjoying our conversation, and I was super curious about something.

"What do you think about the origin of the universe?" I asked him at one point.

"It started with a big bang," he explained confidently, launching into an in-depth explanation of the explosion, gravitational pull, dark matter, and some connected theories.

"Where did that explosion come from?" I asked, deciding I was going to keep working backwards.

The man nodded. "It came from gasses that were contracting and other galaxies that were exploding and forming," he said as he began tracing the chain of events that led up to the explosion.

Gently, I kept asking him where that all came from, trying to see how far back he would trace everything. I thought sooner or later he'd come to the end and have to acknowledge that something was there first.

But the man didn't lose confidence in his explanation, answering each question. "But what's the bottom line?" I asked. "Where did it come from? Where did it all start?"

I'll never forget his answer.

"Helium," he said.

"Helium," I replied.

The man nodded.

"That's interesting. I can't say I've ever heard that before," I said.

"Yes, helium."

"So, tell me more about helium," I asked. The man started to describe its properties as a basic element for all the elements of the universe and how somehow it had existed long before all the others. I pondered what I had just heard. "Where did the helium come from?" I asked.

"Well, that's what we don't exactly understand yet," he admitted. "I just believe it's true."

"Oh, so it's a faith thing," I said. He nodded.

After a moment of reflection, I asked, "What would you think about the idea of a theistic approach, where perhaps there's a supreme being involved?" I made a point to not mention the Bible or Jesus or anything about Christianity yet. "You know, a God who created it, who keeps it in order, who intelligently designed things."

I could tell the man was instinctively beginning to checkout. His expression changed, and he was politely nodding his head, his cynicism evident.

"It sounds like you've heard this before."

"Yeah, I was raised in all that nonsense. I was raised in church. I heard all that creation stuff," he said.

"I am just curious," I asked, "At what point did you turn your back on a God who through intelligent design created everything we see and don't see and embrace helium as the origin of all things?"

I will never forget his answer. "When I was a kid, my dad ran off and left our family poor. My mom took us all to church every Sunday, and she put money in the offering plate faithfully. But one day, the pastor ran off with the money and the secretary," he said. "And since then, I've wanted nothing to do with Christianity."

In that moment, I felt the deep pain and bitterness of his experience with someone who failed to represent God's kingdom with integrity. My heart hurt for this man's heart.

People reject God's wisdom and embrace worldly knowledge or some other substitute for a lot of reasons. This is what John Eldrige calls "The Message of the Arrows" in his book *Sacred Romance*. "At some point we all face the same decision—what will we do with the Arrows we've known? Maybe a better way to say it is, what have they tempted us to do? However they come to us, whether through a loss we experience as abandonment or some deep violation we feel as abuse, their message is always the same: Kill your heart. Divorce it, neglect it, run from it, or indulge it with some anesthetic (our various addictions). Think of how you've handled the affliction that has pierced your own heart. How did the Arrows come to you? Where did they land? Are they still there? What have you done as a result?"

For the man on the plane, it was an old hurt, a grudge against a God who would allow those things to happen that set him on a path void of wisdom. He imagined God to be indifferent and cruel, and so he rejected this version of God that I was suggesting. Yet he, like all of us, had to believe something. The universe couldn't just be empty. He had to have some explanation for life, so he chose … helium.

As knowledgeable as the man was about so many things, he might have been missing wisdom because he was now avoiding the One who supplies it. He was going to find his own way. Like so many, he came to the conclusion that he was alone in the world to figure it out for himself. What happens when we choose knowledge instead of wisdom? True wisdom comes from God; and if you're not willing to consult the Author or have anything to do with Him, settling for knowledge seems like a decent trade. But knowledge has a limited shelf life. It doesn't last. It changes constantly as information and culture change. On the other hand, that hot stove could be yesterday or a thousand years ago and wisdom still works.

Wisdom is unchanging. It is pure gold.

WISDOM IS LIKE GOLD

The pursuit of wisdom is tied to recognizing its value.

In Proverbs 3, we're told that the person who finds godly wisdom and gains understanding is happy, but it goes further than just happiness. In verse 15, God makes it clear that nothing you could possibly want or desire can compare with wisdom. No riches and no experiences come close.

Many people settle for common sense instead of wisdom.

Common sense seems like wisdom. We roll our eyes when people make foolish choices and chalk them up to lacking common sense. In fact, that's originally what the phrase meant. A common body of knowledge that everybody agreed upon. But that's more and more rare these days. Common sense isn't deep wisdom. At best, it's pragmatic. Unlike wisdom, which is unshakable and unmoving, common sense shifts with the situation.

Wisdom is deep and profound, even if it seems deceptively simple. It is uncommon. Wisdom is information that leads to application that leads to life transformation. Proverbs 2:4 says that we should seek wisdom the same way we'd dig for gold or silver. That tells me that:

Wisdom isn't casually lying around, easy to find.

Wisdom is valuable and worth seeking out.

Yet wisdom isn't impossibly complicated. The Gospel writers tell us repeatedly that the poor and the broken heard Jesus gladly. Jesus told us that it is simple enough that even a child can understand and grasp His kingdom.

There's a tension there.

The ability to understand is tied to a sense of humility, a recognition that the God of the universe knows the best way to run His universe. That should give us pause. It might be what God was after when He asked Job the question we mentioned in the last chapter, "Where were you when I laid the foundation of the earth? Tell me, if you have understanding" (Job 38:4 ESV). God didn't ask the question because He wanted to know the answer. He was trying to get Job to see things from a different perspective. His wisdom is what works best in the world He created to run according to His infinite understanding.

So, do you come into alignment with Him, or do you try to force Him into alignment with yourself? And do you wait to pursue wisdom for some later date, or do you pursue it right now?

The Time to Get Wisdom Is Right Now

There's a temptation to put off important things until later.

"When the moment of testing comes, I'll step up and have wisdom in that moment," we tell ourselves, using that as an excuse to cheat on what we think are unimportant things. We might ignore wisdom here and there for a little pleasure for now. "I'll get wisdom later," we reassure ourselves as we pursue worldly success or decide we'd like to experience a few things on our own.

In Luke 16:10, Jesus said that if you're faithful in the small things, you'll be faithful in the big things. But if you are not faithful in the small things, you certainly won't be faithful when the big things come along. Wisdom might be difficult to come by later if you're not pursuing it now.

The world makes pursuing wisdom difficult because it tells you other things are more pressing or more valuable.

Yet, hoping we'll be strong and in a good position when the time comes is not pursuing wisdom; it's gambling (and you might lose). Proverbs 24:10 says that "if we fail in the moment of adversity, our strength is small." Foundations are put under a house for a reason. They are there to support the house should the earth move. Why would the earth move, you ask? In Matthew 7:24 Jesus mentioned a man who had built his house upon the rock; when the storm had passed, his place was still standing. Jesus called him a wise man. Having a foundation of wisdom, one built on truth and integrity right now before the storm hits, matters.

As I said earlier, our culture values many things that are temporal or fleeting. It values beauty, money, and big numbers.

Our culture defines success by how well you score on that list. Whatever else you get, the world tells you, get lots of stuff. Get a big house. Get a big bank account. Get lots of followers. Get a big church. Get fit and beautiful. Get this success now.

And if possible, avoid pain at all costs.

Our culture wants you to delay the pursuit of wisdom so you can pursue those other things. Comfort is king. We're angry about the trash floating by our perfect lives because it makes us uncomfortable. Getting it out of our sight is the most important thing, so we're not reminded of the pain for the moment. Godly wisdom often doesn't seem to make sense because sometimes that pursuit brings trials with it.

Testing and trials are seen as weakness or failure when comfort and success are the governing values. But God encourages us that wisdom is well worth the search and, when we find her, that we must hold onto her for dear life. She is a foundation that will be there when the earth moves.

Our faith grows beautifully when it's founded on godly wisdom. In James 1:3, we're told that the testing of our faith is what gives us the strength to continue. 1 Peter 1:7 tells us our tested faith is worth more than gold.

The Millennium Tower in San Francisco is gorgeous. It opened in 2009, a state-of-the-art 58-story building with luxury apartments and incredible views of the city and the bay. It's the tallest residential building in San Francisco, its glittery glass exterior easily reflecting the sun great distances.

One morning in 2018, building residents heard popping sounds at night. Several woke up to find their windows cracked and shattered glass fallen to the sidewalk below.

Millennium Tower was slowly sinking and tilting.

Come to find out, the building wasn't correctly anchored to the bedrock 250 feet below ground. As beautiful as the building appeared, in time, it started to fail. The building has settled ten inches, and efforts to secure the building with additional pilings have been ongoing. While there were more problems than just broken glass, it was the cracking windows that made people aware there was an issue.

In life, it's not about whether the earth will move under your feet. It's a question of when.

Does it feel like you keep replacing the windows in your life?

Do you keep emptying the trash out of the river?

Maybe you need to dig deeper and get down to your foundation to see what you've built your life on. If your windows in life keep breaking, perhaps it's time to take a close look at what's below ground.

> IN LIFE, IT'S NOT ABOUT WHETHER THE EARTH WILL MOVE UNDER YOUR FEET. IT'S A QUESTION OF WHEN.

CHAPTER THREE REFLECTIONS:
BUILDING SOLID FOUNDATIONS AND PATHS TO HEALING

1) How would you describe some of the foundational aspects of your life? What are some truths or values deep inside of you that have sustained you when life shifted or moved unexpectedly? What did the storm look like? An illness? An unforeseen tragedy? A deep disappointment?

2) Are there patterns of pain or dysfunction that seem to come around on a regular basis? What do they look like, and what do they provoke in you? How much energy do they consume?

3) Who or what would you need with you to take the journey upstream to see where the root causes of these things lie? A trusted friend? New information? A wise and experienced guide?

CHAPTER FOUR

We Need a Guide

*"The real heroes of the Himalayas are
not the mountaineers but the Sherpas!"*
– Mehmet Murat ildan

*"People ruin their lives by their own foolishness
and then are angry at the Lord."*
– Proverbs 19:3 (NLT)

The weather had been overcast and chilly for most of the week; but that morning, thankfully, the sun was shining. There wasn't a cloud in the sky, and a light breeze moved the air just enough to keep the bugs away. It was going to be a gorgeous day. You and your friends have a ten-mile hike planned today, one you've all been looking forward to; and you're relieved the weather is going to cooperate.

Everyone piles into their vehicles and meets in the parking lot at the trailhead as planned. Each has a day pack with water and snacks, a few have walking sticks, and it seems like everything is in order. Since you're in charge of the hike, you go to the ranger station near the trailhead and ask for a map. As exciting as the hike has been to plan, none of your group actually knows the trail well.

"Why do you want a map?" the ranger asks.

That seems like a strange question. "I don't want us to get lost," you reply.

You want a map to guide you so that the hike doesn't go poorly. You want it to go well for everyone, ending with smiles instead of frantic phone calls and rescue helicopters and running from bears.

It's smart to get a map before you start your hike. It's even smarter to be in a place in life that you know you need one. One of the things that always surprises me is how people, particularly those who are younger, are hesitant to ask more questions. We live in a social media age where everyone is an expert, and we are shamed for not knowing the answers. Many will often just fake it. Asking questions, however, is a mark of humility. By asking, I am admitting there are things I don't know; and I am willing to take the position of a learner. Right there we find grace waiting for us.

HAVING THE RIGHT POSTURE

What often gets us lost in the mountains is stubbornness.

We think we can wing it, that we can feel our way along and figure it out as we go. Even if we find ourselves lost, we still feel like we can find our way back if we just trust our own gut instincts.

You cannot be your own guide.

It sounds obvious, but not everyone understands this. The world suggests we go by our feelings and instincts, relying on ourselves and our own sense of direction. We're told that our internal inclination of what's right and wrong will be fine for navigating life.

One of the things I look at before I start a hike is the trailhead map. It's especially useful if I'm on a trail that intersects with another trail. That map tells me two important things: where I am right now, and where will this path take me.

I need to know where I am right now. What feels like facing west might be facing north. Sometimes the clouds block out the sun, or I'm exhausted and lose my sense of direction. Twists and turns and switchbacks have confused me.

I can't totally trust my instincts.

I can't totally trust my feelings.

Self-confidence is a wonderful virtue in most cases, but this time it could deceive me and be my undoing. Just because I sincerely feel I'm on the right path doesn't make it so. It's helpful to have a map that shows me where I am in relation to my destination. It forces me to consider that destination and make sure I'm pursuing the right thing. Humility is a posture that readily admits there are things I might not know,

> IF YOU UNDERSTAND THAT YOU NEED A GUIDE TO CREATE A LIFE THAT WORKS, THAT YOU CAN'T GO THROUGH LIFE ALONE BASED ON INSTINCT AND IN-THE-MOMENT DECISIONS, YOU'RE OFF TO A GOOD START.

and I need help in finding the right path. If you understand that you need a guide to create a life that works, that you can't go through life alone based on instinct and in-the-moment decisions, you're off to a good start. It's okay that you're not an expert on every trail; that's why maps and guides exist. But they aren't of much use if you don't think you need them.

Signs Are Only Useful If You Follow Them

Signs are only good for people interested in going the right direction. All the signs in the world, all the lights and sirens you could put on them, won't do a bit of good if someone has no interest in listening to them.

Imagine you're on a trail, the one marked on your map, the one the ranger gave you. Things have been going well; but suddenly, as you come upon a switchback in the trail, you see evidence of a shortcut. People who hiked earlier saw how much time it would take to use the switchback on the trail map; and they decided to take a shortcut to save time, wearing a dirt path down the steep hillside. But next to that faint trail is a sign that says, "Please Stay On The Marked Trail."

If you care that they're trying to restore the vegetation in the area to cut down on erosion, you'll follow the sign. But if you don't care, the sign has no power to stop you.

Think of the speed limit signs along the roads and the number of people who have blown by them without a thought. Our cities have come up with a clever invention to slow down uncaring people: red light cameras. These are pretty effective at slowing us down, but why? If we are honest, it's not because our hearts have changed; it's because we value what's in our wallets! That is a laymen's example of behavior modification.

When Jesus came as the promised Messiah, the Pharisees couldn't see it. Despite all the signs in the Old Testament that clearly pointed to Him, despite the things He taught and the miracles He did, their pride kept them from seeing the signs.

The Pharisees and religious leaders of Jesus's day were blind to who He was because that's what pride does. It blinds us. It causes us to do things that are irrational, foolish, and destructive because we can't see what's right in front of us, what's looming ahead on the bad path we've taken.

And it's that same pride that tells us that we don't need a guide because we can make it through life alone.

Pride Keeps You Going It Alone

In the Old Testament, rabbis had followers and followers had rabbis. You couldn't call yourself a disciple if you weren't following someone. You couldn't be a disciple in isolation. Paul told his son in the faith, Timothy, that what he had heard from Paul, Timothy was to entrust to faithful men who would in turn teach others. A good guide helps his followers stay on the path, and they in turn help those coming behind them.

But there's another reason you can't do life alone. Remember, we don't live in a morally neutral universe. The playing field of our world is tilted in a certain direction. The world wants to shape you to its image and conform you to its standard. The dynamic of discipleship, according to Romans 12:2, is to not be conformed to the world; Instead, it is to renew your mind so that you can walk a different path.

So, what do we make of this instruction to renew our minds? The core principle of renewal is repentance, embracing a different way of thinking and swallowing our pride to do so.

Authentic discipleship always involves some level of confrontation: both internally to thoughts that aren't true, and externally as our Guide instructs us in the way we should go. If we don't like confrontation, or if we think we can't be wrong, we'll avoid the pain of discipleship and choose comfort as our driving value. Tony Robbins tells us, one of the fundamental motivators of change is that the pain of remaining where I am becomes more unbearable than the pain of moving forward. Life and growth always involve some measure of discomfort. Or as Max Dupree put it, "We cannot become what we want by remaining what we are."

Going through life without a guide who confronts wrong behavior is comfortable until suddenly it isn't. When we hear that iron sharpens iron (Proverbs 27:17), we nod and think it's wise to have friends that keep us on our toes.

Have you ever stopped to think about what that looks like?

Iron on iron causes friction. There's heat and sparks. A dull blade is a dangerous one, so somewhere in that sharpening is a dull blade capable of harm. A knife is only as good as the steel it's made of, and the only thing capable of sharpening it is something harder than that steel. Good news: the Word of God is sharper than any two-edged sword (Hebrews 4:12). It's what will sharpen and pierce us the most, cutting down to the truth. And sometimes God sends a friend who is a true friend, who is mildly abrasive in their truth-telling because they love us. It's what we need to stay on the path.

But in a culture that celebrates independence, we tend not to listen. We avoid admitting we're wrong, and we think we're above correction. We walk away from the sharpening that happens in discipleship and instead choose to surround ourselves with people who think like we do, who confirm our biases, and who will not confront our leanings regardless of how off we may be. We only hear what we want to hear, and our lives are lived out in an echo chamber.

When people come to me for counseling, struggling in some area of their life, I often have a conversation that goes something like this:

"You're thirty years old. Do you remember what your life was like when you were fifteen?" I ask.

"Oh, it was awful. I was so young and immature, and I made some terrible choices," they reply.

"Can you imagine what it would be like if your thirty-year-old self could go back and have a talk with your fifteen-year-old self?"

"That would be incredible! I could save myself so much grief."

"Do you think your fifteen-year-old self would listen?" I ask.

Pause. "Probably not."

"Now imagine if your forty-five-year-old self from the future could come back here, right now, and have a talk with your thirty-year-old self … What would forty-five-year-old you say to you now?"

Same question, same long pause. The true answer sits in the air, hard to admit out loud. So I continue. "If you're not willing to listen to your future forty-five-year-old self, why do you think that might be?" I ask.

Whenever I have this conversation, it's interesting because everyone gets it. They immediately recognize how foolish they were when they were younger. But they don't want to admit that, if they still aren't willing to listen now … doesn't that mean they're still foolish?

The problem isn't that we don't have a guide or don't have the opportunity for a guide. It's that we struggle to be listeners and learners. This is our common malady as fallen human beings. This is the reason for the drastic rise in the tribalism that we see in our public square where people simply shout louder at each other instead of stopping to really see and hear the other person. Listening, really listening to actually know and understand the person speaking to me, is a lost art today. The result is an increasingly isolated existence. Is it any wonder that loneliness is seen as the great health epidemic of our times? Who do we let into those sacred, inner spaces of our lives?

Trusting a Guide Means Admitting You Have Weaknesses

Many ships were taken down because of the irresistible siren call.

In Greek mythology, the sirens were human-like creatures whose voices had incredible power. Just hearing them made people lose their minds and become incapable of rational thought. In the myth, Odysseus, the hero, badly wanted to hear their voices; but he knew that doing so would put him, his crew, and his ship in danger. The sirens would lure them towards the rocks and destroy them.

His solution was to put wax in the ears of his crew, making sure they could not hear the sirens. Then he instructed his men to tie him to the mast of the ship so he couldn't harm himself or anyone else. He ordered them to ignore anything he said and that under no condition were they to change course. They were to stay steady and true on the right heading. He also told them to be ready to attack him with their swords if he managed to escape the ropes.

The ship approached the island where the sirens were, and soon he went insane. His mind and senses were overtaken, and he was powerless to resist their call. He struggled and did everything he could to break free of his ropes and jump into the water, even though that would mean his death. In his confused mind, though, he was sure he would not die but would join the sirens. In time, out of range of the sirens, Odysseus regained his mind; and the ship and crew, having stayed the course, were spared. His commitment to trust his friends saved his life and theirs.

What's the siren song of our culture?

You worked hard, so you deserve a break and a reward. You don't have to put up with inconvenience. You have a right to be happy. You have to look out for yourself, you know. If it feels right, do it. Live in the moment.

The heart wants what the heart wants, essentially; and madness compounds into madness. The ship runs aground.

Many lives have been taken down because of the irresistible siren call.

Part of the humility necessary to accept guidance is to admit that, without help, we have weaknesses that will take us down. That level of honesty is crucial to staying on the right path, but it's not easy. Our culture celebrates power and strength, not weakness. Yet, the best way we can make our life a blessing not only to ourselves but to those around us is to take a posture of humility: being willing to admit weakness, pay attention to signs, and take correction when it's called for.

We joke about how men don't stop and ask for directions or read instructions. (Maybe they were the target audience for the quick guides we now find in every new electronic device.) But the joke has an undercurrent of frustration. How many trips were made much longer, if they were made at all, because someone wouldn't pick up a map or use the GPS on their phone? How many IKEA cabinets are sitting in homes waiting for that one last t-shirt to collapse the drawer because the instructions weren't followed?

Your friends will be thankful that you weren't too proud to stop at the ranger station to get a map because that's an indicator that you want everyone to have an enjoyable day on the trail. You don't want the day to end with a dramatic rescue by the Forest Service or by spending the night in the cold darkness listening to wild animals and wondering where you took a wrong turn.

Observing Human Nature

I have an incredible memory of the first time I ever attended a college football game with my son. It was a bright, sunny fall afternoon. While we were in line to get into the stadium, I noticed a massive line of people off to the right. They were waiting their turn to talk to someone at a table.

"What is that?" I asked my son. I noticed that each person who left the table had a nice Oregon State t-shirt in hand. "Are they giving away t-shirts? I'm going to go grab one!"

While my son stayed in line, I walked over to the table. It wasn't long before I struck up a conversation with the guy in front of me and asked about the t-shirt.

"Yeah, I'm getting a free shirt," he said. "If you sign up for a credit card, they'll give you a shirt."

I was struck by the not-so-subtle strategy of the moment. Someone in a front office somewhere had a genius idea. Here were hundreds of brand-new college freshmen baited with the offer of a free shirt in exchange for signing up for a credit card they probably didn't need. The higher-ups knew something about those students. They knew they could bank on the students' inexperience—what they didn't know about life in the real world—and exploit it for profits. How many students lined up to get a shirt because their friends did? How many questioned the wisdom of doing so but shoved that aside when peer pressure won?

When my sons had their first credit cards, I was pretty insistent that they be careful not to miss the payment deadlines. When we miss those, the late fees are a shocking reminder of how life works. On one occasion, we had a conversation with a banker who patiently explained how the system really worked; and as we walked out, I knew my son had learned something valuable. Those same men, older and more experienced, are now navigating adult life with a healthy understanding of how finances work. Like many of us, they may not know everything there is to know about the inside dealing of the finance world; but they know what does and doesn't work! It's not a crime to be inexperienced, but it might be a vulnerability. The right guide at the right moment can prove to be pivotal in life. How many of those young college students who walked away with a "free" t-shirt ended up later with far more credit card debt than they could have seen coming?

You might be thinking that in the grand scheme of things a t-shirt and a credit card are not going to sink the ship. But what about the bigger tests like the temptation to do a shady business deal or the urge to flirt with that married coworker? Who do you have in your life to whom you have given permission to ask you the tough questions and to whom you're committed to tell the truth and listen to their advice? This is a game changer in a world where the stakes can go up quickly and there is no end to attractive offers. Doing life without a guide is treacherous. Remember, that free t-shirt line wasn't a neutral situation. It was predatory. It was slanted in a particular direction. It was an enticing mixture of psychology, materialism, and opportunity all rolled into one; and it pushed all the right buttons in the moment.

Our current culture is an anxious culture. It's marked by fear of what others think, fear of missing out, fear of being less. So we try harder, spend more, and run faster in hopes of keeping up. Social media is the perfect tool for feeding this beast. In the beginning, it might feel exciting. The adrenaline rush gives us the illusion that we are gaining ground, but it doesn't take long until exhaustion sets in and you can begin to feel it deep in your soul. God, however, offers to graciously lead us in paths of peace. The difference between the two is stark.

Remember the story of the young man who came to me for counseling and admitted that being a Christian wasn't something he thought of as being part of his everyday life? At that moment, I realized that for him, *Christian* was a noun, not a verb. It was a label he wore. It's a t-shirt you put on, a voting bloc, just another religious tag.

But in the New Testament, we're called to be followers. That's active. Christianity is a verb, because it's a question of who you are following. Who is your guide? Who are you letting speak into your life? Whose voice do you listen to?

Hearing The Voice of Your Guide

In Proverbs 8 and 9, Lady Wisdom goes to the highest place in town. Where does Lady Folly go?

The same place.

The same strategic, high-vantage point place. Both of them are calling out, beckoning to the undecided, telling them which route to go. But they can't both be right. Lady Folly has her own map, and she's happy to show you that the route she has planned for you is shorter and easier and without consequence.

"Look at my map," she says. "You deserve a break. You work hard. You can afford to lighten up, to loosen up. This is such an easier path."

Wisdom and Folly both want your attention. They'd both love to be your guide. Discernment plays a big part in choosing which path you will take.

> THE VOICE OF GOD COMES TO US FIRST IN HIS WORD. SECONDLY, IT COMES THROUGH THE HOLY SPIRIT. AND THIRDLY, HE OFTEN WILL USE OTHERS TO SPEAK TO US.

Jesus said He was the good shepherd and that His sheep would know His voice (John 10:11–18). He is the perfect guide, but how do we know if we know His voice? How do we know we're not listening to a mockingbird, something mimicking the sound of Jesus's voice?

That's the ten-thousand-dollar question.

The voice of God comes to us first in His Word. Secondly, it comes through the Holy Spirit. And thirdly, He often will use others to speak to us. Proverbs calls that wise counsel. But if

I flip that order around and listen to others first, before God's Word and His Holy Spirit, it can be very dangerous.

The Secret Service is tasked by the government to spot fake currencies. They build their skills by carefully studying all the features of real money in order to recognize a counterfeit bill when they see one. Being very familiar with the real thing is the best way to know when something fake comes along. When Jesus says His sheep hear His voice, that tells us that we need to get used to what His voice really sounds like.

That happens by reading and spending time in the Word of God. If you don't know where to begin, start with the Gospels. Listen to what Jesus has to say and watch how He deals with the wide range of humanity and life's circumstances. He said, "He that has seen me has seen the Father" (John 14:9). You're seeing God at work. Above all, keep in mind His life mission as stated in John 10:10, "I have come that you might have life and life abundantly." The Word of God informs us of the ways of God, taking out the guesswork that happens when we're trying to listen to others or go it on our own.

If we don't read what God has to say, we're completely untethered, susceptible to other voices. The Sirens will find us an easy target. Lady Folly will continue to play us over and over. Ironically, we often end up confused and angry that our Guide isn't helping us out when the real problem is we can't discern His voice.

And that's when it's so easy to say, "If God won't tell me what to do, I'll just figure it out on my own."

USING THE RIGHT GUIDE

An old trail ranger who had mastered every trail in the area sat down with paper and pencil. He had been retired for nearly two years, yet he still remembered the placement of every tree and rock after spending decades maintaining the trail system.

"You're going to want to hike down the hill and cross over until you get to the rock formation," he said as he sketched out a detailed map. "Once there, turn to the south. That trail will loop around and bring you safely home."

The ranger's map was detailed. The ranger was confident. He'd hiked that path a thousand times and knew what he told you was good. But what was supposed to be a short hike turned into an all-day hike. You followed the guide, but it took you a different way.

What the ranger didn't know was that in the few years since he'd been on the job, the trail had been changed. The guide you had was really good at one time; but in the here and now, he nearly got you lost. The game had changed, and your guide hadn't.

A good guide that guides you wrongly is actually a bad guide.

The best guide is one that is there with you on the journey. Life is complicated, difficult, and ever changing; and it's not enough to have a guide who talks you through it from a distance. If that old ranger had gone hiking with you that day, he'd have seen the right way to go. It's one thing to talk to a guide on the other side of the desk, but something else to have one who will go with you. This is why in the book of Proverbs, wisdom is personified. She is not just an accumulation of knowledge or information. Those can be deceptive measurements of our lives. Lady Wisdom is someone who offers to go with you in the journey and be with you in the moments when you need her most.

There are lots of helpful guides out there. There are powerful speakers and helpful books written by people with good intentions. They've used a certain path to great success, and they share it with you in the hopes that you'll see the same result.

But they are not your Creator. God knows you better than anyone else, and the wisdom in His Word is always true at any time for anyone who will believe it. Even better, He is with you each step of the way.

Who are you letting guide you through life? Do you choose a guide simply by their outward results in hopes of getting the same? Are they promising you freedom with all kinds of wonderful words and ideas, while they themselves are stuck in a depraved life that doesn't work (2 Peter 2:19)?

It's not only who you let guide you on the trail, but who you're bringing along for the journey. Your trail mates have voices, too; and we need to be vigilant that we are all of one heart in finding the path that leads to life.

We need a guide, the right guide; so let's be wise about who we travel with.

CHAPTER FOUR REFLECTIONS:
NAVIGATING GOOD COUNSEL AND TRUE GUIDANCE

1) As I look around my life, who do I have near me that I can trust to help me make wise life decisions? When have they given me timely counsel, and what did they see that perhaps I did not? What did they have that I lacked?

2) Am I asking the right people the right questions? Is there someone near me who has life experience or perspective that I lack or need in my life right now? What kind of questions might I ask them that would unlock their wisdom and experience for my benefit?

3) Social media is full of all kinds of information. How is a mentoring relationship different from simply sifting through facts and advice to answer my questions or give me guidance?

CHAPTER FIVE

It Matters Who You Go With

*"Show me your friends and
I'll show you your future."*
– John C. Maxwell

*"Become wise by walking with the wise; hang out
with fools and watch your life fall to pieces."*
– Proverbs 13:20 (MSG)

*"And if the blind lead the blind
they both fall into the ditch."*
– Matthew 15:14 (MSG)

Unlike water, fire flows uphill.

It's not something I knew as a twelve-year-old kid; but it is one of those things that once I learned it, I really, really learned it.

We had four players. We had the baseball. We had the bat. We had our gloves. We just needed to define the playing field in that old vacant lot.

Standing at the edge of the grass, plenty of space stretching before us, we were silent. Before we could get in any game play, we'd have to lay out some bases and scuff the grass first. It was a hot, clear day; and the sun beat down on us, making sweat pool under our caps. Building a ball diamond didn't sound like fun.

It was as if we were all waiting for one of the others to do something first, to come up with a plan or call the game.

"Let's burn the baselines," one blurted out.

I would never have come up with it on my own. (Of course, if I'd been alone, I wouldn't have been playing baseball, either.) Even if the thought had wandered briefly through my mind, I'd definitely never have gone through with it by myself. But to our twelve-year-old ears, with three other companions nearby, it didn't sound so terrible at the time. The minute the words rang out, they rang true.

We got a can of gasoline and poured as straight of a trail as we could to make the baselines. One friend stood where he thought the base should go; and another, hunched over, poured gas out of the heavy can trying to control the flow. When he got to where home would be, he set the can down.

"Who has the matches?" he asked. It was a hot day, and the gas was evaporating. My friend pulled out a match from the box and lit it. The flickering flame was small, but not for long. He tossed it on the ground where we'd started to pour the gas. The flame quickly grabbed hold of the gas, and it raced around the infield just like we planned. Rounding first base, then sliding into second, taking a sharp left, and rushing to third base. It was awesome to watch, and we were hollering and cheering at our genius.

The fire raced towards home plate.

Home base, where we'd left the gas can.

In our mind, the fire would stay in a controlled burn, following the lines we'd set out for it and stopping at the end of the pour. We didn't have the experience to know the physics of flammable liquids, of fumes, of how fire could run uphill and back into gas cans.

Our happiness turned to horror as we watched the flame leap like a gymnast from the ground into the gas can, running uphill and outside of the boundaries we'd set for it.

BOOM!

The gas can was shredded in all directions, bits of metal whizzing by our heads. The heat was intense, a wave of warmth so sudden I reached up to feel if my eyebrows were still on my face. It felt like the sun fell out of the sky for just a moment and landed on us.

It was the biggest explosion I'd seen, and it's a small miracle that we weren't hurt.

How could the four of us, a solid majority, have been wrong? We'd all agreed it was a great idea. And yet, it really, really wasn't.

The crowd doesn't always make the right decision. Sometimes it makes the wrong one in a big, spectacular, messy way. That's why it matters who you travel with.

WE ARE A PRODUCT OF INFLUENCE

We were designed for influence, both to influence others and to be influenced. We are all a combination of the influential people in our lives.

That asks us to answer a question: who do you let influence you? Who has had a hand in shaping you?

We want to conform.

We want to be accepted.

We want to fit in.

We don't want to have to fight to decide what we know to be right or what we will do if it's in conflict with the people around us. The people who influence us have the power to turn our lives in a direction we might not otherwise want to go.

> WE WERE DESIGNED FOR INFLUENCE, BOTH TO INFLUENCE OTHERS AND TO BE INFLUENCED. WE ARE ALL A COMBINATION OF THE INFLUENTIAL PEOPLE IN OUR LIVES. THAT ASKS US TO ANSWER A QUESTION: WHO DO YOU LET INFLUENCE YOU?

The Foolishness of the Crowd

Consider ants, which are hive-mind creatures.

The Bible applauds their example when it comes to being a worker. But house hunting with ants makes for an eye-opening revelation. Uppsala University in Sweden and Arizona State University decided to use ants to find out if the wisdom of the crowd is better than the wisdom of an individual, and the results were surprising.[1]

Ants tend to do everything as a group, so researchers set up a scenario where they had to move from where they currently lived to a new location. They had the option of either a light colored or darker colored piece of hollowed wood. Ants would naturally choose the darker color because it would be safer and offer more camouflage.

But in the study, those busy, instinctive ants didn't always make the right choice. If a larger number of ants ventured to the lighter wood first they "convinced" more ants to come over and make that selection. Ants actually recruited other ants to come over to the inferior new home simply because the numbers already there convinced them it must be the best choice. Ultimately, all of the ants ended up with the worst house on the block.

When faced with an unknown or overwhelmed by too many options, it's easier to rely on the decisions of the greatest number of people around us.

Because surely everyone can't be wrong.

Surely four twelve-year-olds and a gas can wouldn't make a bad decision, not if all four decided it was the right

---

[1] "The Stupidity of the Crowd." The Atlantic. Accessed November 30, 2023. Available online: https://www.theatlantic.com/health/archive/2013/07/the-stupidity-of-the-crowd/278188/.

thing to do. Surely my good friends who say they like me wouldn't make decisions that could bring me harm.

Yet, even when faced with better options, we can make the foolish choice for no other reason than that the people around us have made the same one. We'll conform, obey, persuade ourselves, concede our identities, turn into passive observers instead of active participants, or join a faceless, out-of-control mob, all because we assume that the crowd possesses wisdom we couldn't possibly have on our own. We'll collaborate instead of flexing the creativity and minds God gave us, unaware that research has shown working together with the crowd can reduce our creative output.[2]

In a world where we hear everyone's opinions, where collaboration is praised and groupthink is quietly demanded, the wisdom of the crowd seems impossible to deny.

But the majority can be wrong.

The Power of Social Influence

Proverbs 6 tells us what God hates, and we could think of it as a handy list of what kind of person makes a bad friend.

According to the list, someone you should avoid is a person who is proud. They tell lies, purposefully harm the innocent, and come up with schemes to cheat and do violence to others. They are quick to rush into what is evil, making a

---

[2] "Want To Be More Productive And Creative? Collaborate Less" Fast Company. Accessed November 30, 2023. Available online: https://www.fastcompany.com/3063787/want-to-be-more-productive-and-creative-collaborate-less.

habit of slandering or gossiping about others; and they create and feed conflict in the community, sometimes disguising it as just being a straight shooter.

God hates those things, and anyone who does these things should not be in your close circle.

"I would never have a friend who did all of those things!" you might think, assured that you'd be able to spot such things easily.

Have you ever viewed what you see on social media in light of that list?

Nearly three quarters of all Gen Z and Millennials follow social media influencers, with half of all Millennials trusting what those influencers recommend.[3]

Who is influencing you? You might not think of your favorite social media influencers, or even your own social media followers and friends, as part of the group who is traveling with you through life. But they are.

Because of social influence, we don't always do the things we want to do, the things we know we should do, the things we normally would do. Peer pressure is the phrase we used to use, but it's more than just a bunch of friends pressuring us to do something we wouldn't otherwise do. Because, as it turns out, it doesn't take that much pressure at all.

Hang around stupid people who do stupid things, and you're bound to get in trouble. Our friends have power in our

---

[3] https://blog.hubspot.com/marketing/influencer-marketing-stats.

lives. Proverbs 13:20 says that if we walk with wise people, we grow wise. But when we walk with fools, our life falls to pieces.

There aren't only fools to watch out for. Proverbs 22:24–25 wisely tells us not to even associate with a hot-tempered person or someone who is easily angered because you'll learn their ways and become just like them.

Any bad behavior, in general, is contagious. This is even more true when most of the people around us are a negative influence. According to a neuroscience study, we will change our opinions and how we behave to follow what is considered "normal" by the people around us.[4] Social influence pings the part of our brain associated with processing rewards. We are quick to trust the opinions of those around us and quick to feel confident that we're making the right choices.

Like lighting up a vacant lot.

Mistaking Quantity for Quality

In Proverbs 18:24, we're told that friends come and go, but a true friend sticks by you like family.

In today's culture, we tend to measure things quantitatively. We notice how big something is, how much there is, or how much something costs. The question is always "how much?" or "how many?".

---

[4] Zhenyu Wei, Zhiying Zhao, & Yong Zheng. "Following the Majority Social Influence in Trusting Behavior." Frontiers in Neuroscience, vol. 13, 2019. Accessed November 29, 2023. Available online: https://www.frontiersin.org/articles/10.3389/fnins.2019.00089/full.

"How many people attend your church?" I often hear at conferences. It's not the pastor with 32 people who is asked to speak; it's the pastor with 3200 people.

Unfortunately, we do this with friendship.

"How many followers do you have on Instagram? Facebook? TikTok?"

In the late 1980s, before social media ruled the world, a psychologist named Robin Dunbar did a study and found that, on average, people can handle up to 150 meaningful social relationships at any one point in time.[5] This number became known as "Dunbar's Number," but it's worth noting that not all those 150 relationships were the same in terms of closeness.

The real discovery Dunbar made is that most people can only really manage five close friends. A study in 2020 revealed that, despite the shift in culture toward social media, we haven't changed. Three to five very close friends are all we really need, and all we can really handle.[6] There may be many other people we like. Those are acquaintances; they are not close.

But we still fixate on having more "friends" and wonder how many other people have.

God measures by quality, not quantity. And in God's economy, true friends are much more than a follower on a social media platform, much more than an acquaintance.

---

[5] https://citeseerx.ist.psu.edu/viewdoc/download?doi=10.1.1.464.5806&rep=rep1&type=pdf.

[6] https://onlinelibrary.wiley.com/doi/abs/10.1002/adsp.12086.

Anyone with access to people has influence. That list of 2000 people who follow you on Instagram counts. Because we were designed for influence—to influence others and to be influenced—the collection of people you follow on Instagram has significant power. They might not stick close to you or sharpen you, but they will influence you. And it's easy to be fooled into thinking that having a large number of friends means your crowd will keep you safe.

A true friend is someone who is closer than a brother; proximity matters, so be careful who you pull close.

WHAT MAKES A GOOD FRIEND

What makes a good friend? Doesn't everybody in a lost and hurting world need friends as well, even people who are liars, who stir up conflict, who hurt others, who are angry?

Absolutely. This world is full of people who need friends. Jesus was a friend of sinners, Someone who cared about the broken. But remember that the Jesus who ministered to the multitude had twelve friends He called His disciples. They were invited to be close to Him, walking in a rabbi/student relationship with Him. And even out of those twelve, He seemed to have had an inner circle of three: Peter, James, and John. They were His intimate, closest companions.

Jesus modeled the right approach.

The question isn't whether we can be kind and care about broken people. It's a question of influence. Am I influencing them, or are they influencing me?

A Good Friend Perseveres

A good friend is one who will love at all times, who's there even when things are difficult (Proverbs 17:17). There's a certain kind of friend who helps you persevere and inspires you, and there's a certain kind of person who drains and exhausts you.

As believers, we need to minister to people who are needy, to those who find themselves in a place of misery, or who are slogging along through life's challenges. But you can only be around people like that for measured amounts of time. Misery cannot be your constant companion, your closest friend. Jesus was a man familiar with suffering, but at the end of the day He had His comrades in arms—men who shared the load with Him. We need to be inspired and encouraged and built up. As we pour into others, we must find those who will also pour into us. Ecclesiastes 4:9–10 points out that two people are better than one because they can do more. If one should fall, the other can help her up, while the person who is alone has no one to help them up.

> *AS WE POUR INTO OTHERS, WE MUST FIND THOSE WHO WILL ALSO POUR INTO US.*

A Good Friend Provides Wise Advice

A good friend who truly loves and cares speaks into your life with truth and wisdom, even if it hurts at the time (Proverbs 27).

We tend to gravitate towards comfort, gathering people around us who think like we do to avoid tension. I've watched how the disintegration of the family in our culture has caused us to lose touch with the wisdom of older generations. Newly married couples couldn't find better friends than an older couple who have been through deep waters and made it to the other side. If you're in a rough patch in your marriage because of betrayal, should you go to someone who faced the same thing and walked away? Or the married friend who pushed through? We're not looking for perfect people but tender, humble people.

We need to find friends who offer counsel that's beyond our sphere of understanding.

A Good Friend Will Sharpen You

I have bad news: if you are hardheaded, God, in His great wisdom and mercy, will send someone into your life who is more stubborn than you.

It's not because He's trying to torture you but because He loves you.

A wooden stick can't sharpen a metal blade. Sharpening requires something that's stronger and harder. Anyone who works with knives, whether a chef or a craftsman, will tell you that a dull blade is the most dangerous blade and the most ineffective. A sharp blade gets the job done.

We need friends who sharpen us in the right way, in a way that ultimately helps instead of permanently hurts. We need friends who help stretch our abilities outside of where we're comfortable, who provide honest critique so we grow. They might rub us in a way that feels abrasive at the time, but the sharpening makes us better (Proverbs 27:17).

It's easy to get comfortable in a rut, running on autopilot, surrounding ourselves with friends that don't demand we step up.

If comfort is the governing value in our lives, discipleship goes out the window. Every decision to grow will meet with an excuse and be rejected.

A Good Friend Tells the Truth

A good friend will tell you the truth and hold you accountable.

Proverbs 27:6 says that "wounds from a friend can be trusted, but an enemy multiplies kisses." This verse sounds strange to us because we're a culture that shakes hands. But in many cultures in the world, when you meet someone, you give them a hug or a kiss on the cheek. I've been in meetings where they kissed each other at the door, but the meeting itself was treacherous. They were anything but friends, sniping and arguing during the meeting; but later they gushed about how wonderful or appreciated the other is.

As the saying goes, sometimes the truth hurts. Have you ever been wounded by a friend? If you're true friends, running away and breaking ties isn't an option. The wound of a true friend who speaks the truth can be seen as an act of love. When I preach, I can easily see the people directly in front of me. Thanks to my peripheral vision, I can also see a little on both sides, perhaps about 180 degrees.

But what I can't possibly see is all that is behind me. The other 180 degrees. Those are called blind spots for a reason.

A friend is someone who helps you see the big picture. They make it possible to see the full 360, even if it hurts. Here's a great life question to be asking ourselves. "What part of my life that I cannot see would be helpful to know about in order to live better and love others well?"

THE MOST IMPORTANT DECISION YOU'LL MAKE

I tell people that, outside of where you're going to spend eternity, who you spend this life with is the most important decision you'll make.

If it matters who your friends are in life, it absolutely matters who you marry. Marriage is the deepest and most intimate access that someone can give, a friendship like no other, one with soul ties. Who are you opening your life up to? Who do you open your heart up to? Who have you given access to your life?

Unfortunately, too many people make that decision based on feelings, attractions, and a hurt they are trying to fill. That's why, every forty-two seconds, someone in America gets a divorce.[7,8] Considering the data on how many marriages there are, that means that there are about three divorces in the time it

[7] Wilkinson & Finkbeiner, LLP, "Divorce Statistics and Facts | What Affects Divorce Rates in the U.S.?," 2023, https://www.wf-lawyers.com/divorce-statistics-and-facts/.

[8] In 2019, the CDC released marriage and divorce statistics for the United States. With only 44 states reporting, these numbers are probably higher.

takes a couple to say their wedding vows. In a forty-year period, over two-thirds of all first marriages end in divorce. On average, a first marriage that's headed for divorce will last about eight years.

But there's a bigger problem.

Divorce rates, for the second marriage, jumps from 50 to 56 percent. For the third marriage, it jumps to 73 percent.[9] Why?

Because a wounded person is marrying and remarrying, hoping that this is going to be the one to fix everything, not realizing that if Jesus isn't the One, no one is.

No one gets married planning on splitting up, but splitting up is what seems to happen. The result is a life of pain.

We Weren't Meant to be Pulled Apart

It was God Himself who said it wasn't good for man to be alone.

Eve was like Adam in some ways, having some common characteristics; but she was also very different. So, why did He bring them together when each were unique from the other?

In doing so, He made something entirely new.

The book of Ephesians talks about bringing people together in an attitude of mutual servanthood and humility. That's what God did with Adam and Eve: He brought two

---

[9] Mark Banschick, M.D., "The High Failure Rate of Second and Third Marriages," Psychology Today, February 6, 2012, https://www.psychologytoday.com/us/blog/the-intelligent-divorce/201202/the-high-failure-rate-of-second-and-third-marriages.

people together to make something new, something with incredible beauty and creativity. He combined them body, soul, and spirit in this new thing called "us."

If you're going to be bonded to somebody, if you're going to make a new "us," it would make sense to make sure it's a wise choice. It's like chocolate and milk. Once you mix them together, it's difficult to separate them. This is why God said that what he has joined together, let no man separate.

Sometimes, to illustrate this in teaching sessions, I'll pick up two paper plates and show them to the audience. One will have a photo of a man and the other will have a photo of a woman. Once I'm sure everyone has seen the images, I launch into a detailed discussion about epoxy cement. What's interesting about epoxy is that it's one part resin and one part hardener. These two substances have no sticking power on their own, but when mixed have incredible power to bond two surfaces together. Once it's mixed, there is no going back. The more I talk, the more people in the room get confused.

"What's the science class for?" they wonder.

Then, holding the plate with the face of the man, I'll spread some of the mixture on his face and then some on face of the woman, all while continuing to talk about the miraculous sticking power of the resin and the hardener. As I talk, I press the two plates together face to face. I then do a short explanation on the definition of physical and emotional intimacy.

At some point, after a few minutes, I attempt to pull them apart. It's never a clean break. There are bits and pieces of each of their faces on the other plate. The result is a ragged mess that makes it difficult to make out what the original image of the person looked like. It's a strong visual, and some people will even begin weeping as they realize what breaking up has done to their hearts.

The bond was never meant to come apart. It wasn't designed to be separated.

Breaking up is hard to do because we weren't designed to break up. We get wounded. We can bear a lot of things, but a wounded spirit is hard to bear (Proverbs 18:14).

Out of Two There is One

God is a relational God.

In the first verses of Genesis, we read that He says, "let *us* make." He's a community building God, and when He made man in His image, He said almost right away that it wasn't good for man to be alone. Jesus died to create the Church, made up of a body of believers meant to function together.

For us, He created the idea of marriage where two become one. At a wedding ceremony, I tell the people attending that they are about to witness a miracle. The bride and groom might walk up the aisle as two single individuals; but when we're done, they will walk out as one flesh. A brand new thing has actually been created. The new relationship doesn't promise to always be easy, but it has the potential to shape us like nothing else. It's something sacred and beautiful. What if that's more than metaphorical and is actually a reality? We struggle with this idea of community and relationship coming together to be one for several reasons.

For one thing, our culture is steeped in individualism. We value and champion our personal achievements and freedoms.

"Look at how he pulled himself up by his own bootstraps!"

"See how she has her life together and pays her own bills!"

It has that "I did it my way" feel to it. But where did we get such an idea? Proverbs 1:8 tells us that someone who isolates himself is simply seeking his own desire, and he rages against wise judgment. We stand and fall as individuals, or we run to find the wisdom of crowds. Nowhere, in either action, do we find a communal relationship. I will be the first to admit that there are a lot of things about church culture that can frustrate me. Get up close to people, and it's not long before you begin to notice their flaws. But there is something transformational about binding myself to an authentic and persevering community. It has the power to change me because I not only begin to see other people's flaws but my own as well. In a healthy community, my flaws are not exposed to destroy me but to make me better and in turn make us all better. Maybe that's why Gary Thomas in his book *Sacred Marriage* asks, "What if God didn't give us marriage to make us happy but to make us holy?"

We are not called to live and decide and grow alone. We can't mentor ourselves.

What if the strategy of the enemy is to simply isolate us and get us alone? Someone offends us, so we walk away. We find another friend. We find another church, or we decide to stay home and have church at home, by ourselves. The enemy knows what pushes our personal buttons; and when he gets us alone, we fill the silence with thoughts that are typically awful or negative.

Listen to the tape that's running in your head.

"No one understands you. Nothing will ever change. You don't need this hassle. There is something better out there. Be brave and just cut the ties and leave." Being offended is one of the oldest tricks in the book to get you away from what is best for you.

If you listen to that, you'll end up alone and raging against wisdom, even though God created you to be in relationship with others so you are made stronger (Ecclesiastes 4:12).

It's not just the individualistic push of our culture that makes it difficult to understand how God views relationships. In a culture where we talk so flippantly about love—we love our dog, we love pizza, we love biking—the concept of authentic love in a relationship can lose its meaning. I often hear people say that marriage is "just a piece of paper," but the reluctance for some to actually sign that paper shows that deep down in their hearts they know it's more.

It's a commitment that transcends feelings and emotions and fleeting desires.

It's the plunger that mixes the epoxy and resin together and makes what was two separate people into one. And when people don't understand this and are casual about love and sex and relationships, there are bits and pieces of us all over the place because we're creating faulty bonds.

An Unbreakable Bond in a Broken World

You can have the greatest wood glue on the planet; but any woodworker knows that, even with that going for you, just a little bit of dust or debris between the two pieces of wood will be a problem.

It might seem fine, at first. The bond holds. It might even hold for a while. Everything seems fine. But in a moment of pressure down the road, that joint will come apart right where the dust was that prevented that bond from being clean and enduring.

A clean bond is really hard to accomplish in a broken world, but the good news is that it's possible because I have personally witnessed it in the lives of countless people. It matters who you go with, and it matters who you bond with.

> COMMUNITY IS NOT AN ACTION. IT'S THE RESULT OF ACTION. IT'S THE RESULT OF AUTHENTIC FRIENDSHIPS, WHICH ARE THE RESULT OF TRULY LOVING ONE ANOTHER.

Community is not an action. It's the result of action. It's the result of authentic friendships, which are the result of truly loving one another. So many people want community, but they don't want to learn the behavior that comes with the thing they say they admire. They want to bond, but they don't want to take care of the dust that might get in the way.

God created us to need to be with others, something He intended to strengthen and enhance us. But what was designed to enhance us, when we use it carelessly, now hurts us.

When your car breaks down, do you ask for a dishonest or a trustworthy mechanic? When you're hungry, do you look for a sketchy review or one with five stars? Why do we consider the options so carefully for our car, our hunger, our physical body, but not for our heart? Why don't we guard who we allow inside of our circle?

The world competes for our affection. It longs for our allegiance. It wants a bit of our attention, a piece of our heart, a little here and there. Be a member, join the club, buy the product, look at this—until you don't have anything left to give. But what if we are deliberately designed by God with certain limitations? And by acknowledging those limitations, it actually helps us focus on what we were intended to do and be? Passion by definition is a strong and intense desire toward something or someone. We can't possibly be passionate about dozens of different things or people without becoming a little jaded or indifferent about everything. Maybe that's why the writer of Proverbs 27:20 said "The eyes of man are never satisfied." Maybe that's one reason the wisdom of Proverbs gives way to the cynicism of Ecclesiastes. Solomon's unconstrained heart chased after the collection of wealth, women, and accomplishments that eventually left his family, his kingdom, and even his own heart divided. So, when we think about a life that works, the first question shouldn't be what kind of life we want. It should be who has our hearts.

CHAPTER FIVE REFLECTIONS:
YOUR COMPASS FOR SELF-AWARENESS

1)   If I was to rate my self-awareness on a scale from 1–10, what would I say it is? If I was to ask a friend to honestly rate me, would the numbers be the same? Is there a difference in the numbers, and if so, why might that be?

2)   Who are three people in my life that I would genuinely listen to even if it was tough to hear? Have there been any relationships that have failed because telling or hearing the truth was too painful?

3)   What kind of friend brings life to me? List three things that they do or say that makes me better. How can I be that person to others?

CHAPTER SIX

Stubbornness Is Not Golden

*"What experience and history teaches us is that
people and governments have never learned
anything from history, or acted on principles
deduced from it."*
– Georg Wilhelm Friedrich Hegel

*"The difference between school and life?
In school, you're taught a lesson then given
a test. In life, you're given a test that teaches
you a lesson."*
– Tom Bodet

*"A stubborn fool considers his own way the right
one, but a person who listens to advice is wise."*
– Proverbs 12:15 (GW)

Robert had worked at our church for a few years, helping
with custodial and maintenance work. While he did a good
job, I noticed concerning things about his personality. As
I interacted with him and watched how he was with others,

I saw a harsh and stubborn person at work. He was particularly hard towards his wife.

Berating his wife seemed to flow naturally from Robert, and I could almost see her wilt more each day. The shower of negative and angry words chipped away at her to the point that I don't know how she was able to function with any confidence or joy.

I met with him several times, trying to reason with him about what was going on.

"Listen, Robert, this is what the Word of God says about our attitudes towards those we say we love," I said at our last meeting.

He cut me off. "Wait, you're not going to pull the Bible out on me, are you?"

"Well, Robert, I am not only your boss, but I'm also your pastor and friend; and yes, that's about the best I have. If we take the Bible out of the equation, there's not much to talk about," I said.

"I don't need to hear it. My life is fine."

"If that's the course you're going to take, let me know how it works out," I said, already knowing where his unchanged trajectory would take him.

Unsurprisingly, things didn't work out for him.

His marriage blew up, and his wife divorced him. It was another reminder that, outside of the Word of God, that type of person tends to do what's right in his own eyes (Proverbs 21:2). Later in reflection, I thought that I had no dog in that fight. I wasn't trying to sell him anything that would benefit me personally.

I was just trying to offer him some advice that would have saved him and his family a lot of grief!

If you asked somebody on the street what caused the Titanic to sink, they'd likely tell you it was an iceberg. But the truth is that arrogance and negligence were the root cause. People believed the ship was unsinkable, which kept them from exercising caution in navigation or considering flaws in the design. Add the rest of the errors and assumptions made during that voyage, and the collision with the iceberg was almost inevitable.

In the same way, Robert had a wonderful wife and a potentially wonderful marriage; yet he stubbornly refused to change course and plowed ahead to destruction. It boggles the mind. What's behind it? Why do we do what we do?

THE PROBLEM OF STUBBORNNESS

Stubbornness can sometimes appear to be a virtue; but in most cases, it is the unredeemed version of perseverance. A stubborn heart locks us into a destructive pattern of repeating terrible, painful history because we refuse to think outside of the ruts that have formed in our lives. Soon we find ourselves going against the grain of life. Whether it's a simple Shaker chair, with its clean lines and no-fuss design, or the elaborate carved and curling wood of a Regency chair, the master craftsman who made it understood wood grain.

Every individual tree sprouts and then grows a certain way. That becomes the grain in the wood; and a good craftsman, who later takes that wood to make something beautiful, knows he can't fight the grain. He has to figure out which way it's going, and that's the direction to sand and plane.

Wisdom works in the direction of growth. And when you respect the design of the wood, you can create the thing you intend. When you go against the grain, you get splinters and a surface that fights you the whole way. If you've ever acquired those life splinters, have you stopped to honestly ask yourself how and why they got there? Extracting those splinters can be painful and time consuming! Stubbornness is one of the great mysteries of the human condition.

Going with the grain of life is working in the direction God designed you for. You'll avoid the splinters, but that doesn't mean it's always easy. Going with God's grain often requires you to go against the grain of culture because culture tends to go against the grain of God.

> GOING WITH THE GRAIN OF LIFE IS WORKING IN THE DIRECTION GOD DESIGNED YOU FOR. YOU'LL AVOID THE SPLINTERS, BUT THAT DOESN'T MEAN IT'S ALWAYS EASY. GOING WITH GOD'S GRAIN OFTEN REQUIRES YOU TO GO AGAINST THE GRAIN OF CULTURE BECAUSE CULTURE TENDS TO GO AGAINST THE GRAIN OF GOD.

Our culture beats a drum of being original, being independent—it celebrates you being your own person, as if that is the only way you can be really, truly, you. It even encourages you to go against the design, packaging it as a way to succeed and stand out.

Assert yourself! Leap before you look! Build grit and determination! Refuse to conform! Define life on your terms! Take the road less traveled! Laugh at adversity and embrace the pain that comes from the splinters! You are the master of your own destiny!

That list is exhausting to think about. Ironically, going with God's grain and against the culture's will make you stand out more than anything the culture promises.

But what is the difference between stubbornness and perseverance?

Stubbornness insists that my way is the only way to get where I want to go; it commits to method. Perseverance doesn't commit to method alone but commits to results that produce enduring fruit. Isn't this what Jesus meant when He said, "Those who remain in me, and I in them, will produce much fruit. For apart from me you can do nothing" (John 15:5). The key words there are *remain* and *abide*. To resolve to stay the course together with Him, recognizing that a life that flourishes comes through remaining firmly attached to the vine. If God is the Designer, Creator, and Maintainer of this thing we call life, why would I go against His grain?

Now it's true that throughout the ages the people of God have been called to persevere with a form of "holy stubbornness." I may have to go against the grain of culture in order to stay true to the grain of God's design. It may mean saying I will not bow to the idols or the emperor; I will not call evil good or good evil; I will not compromise the truth or my identity just because it is socially unpopular. For many saints in history, this has looked like standing fast in the face of threats, ridicule, persecution, or even death. This kind of saintly stubbornness has brought suffering for the Kingdom's sake, and it comes with the promise of great reward. "To he who overcomes" is a recurring theme all through the New Testament. But this kind of stubbornness is not rooted in me, but rather in a deep conviction that God is the only wise God and to Him belongs the glory and honor. If we are going to suffer for our faith, let us not suffer for being obnoxious or self-righteous fools, but for being humble and faithful ambassadors of the King. This kind of allegiance trumps all other authorities and has always proven to be an authentic and sometimes irritating witness to a watching world.

Life-giving wisdom then springs from a healthy relationship with our Designer and Creator where He's being allowed to inform our decisions and navigate the waters. He's the master craftsman, and we humbly take the position of the apprentice. Do we really think we could do better apart from Him?

Think of it like the inversion principle. God's grain is the true grain, and what the world offers is its counterfeit. It's a lie, packaged as uniqueness and nonconformity. Going with the grain of the world is going against what God intended, and that's why we get what we sow. Going with the true grain is radical nonconformity.

It's possible that much of what we do could be rooted in ignorance that refuses to look closely and carefully at our steps. Or could it be that there are critical pieces of information missing that would change how we saw things if we were only aware of them?

When we lived in Southern Mexico as missionaries, I had the opportunity to be a guest speaker at a church down the coast from us. I was friends with the pastors at the church, which had a good-sized congregation; and the lead pastor needed someone to fill in. I'd been there before and was happy to help. The associate pastor would be in charge in the lead pastor's absence. The service started with typical pre-service activity, and then we sat down in the front row as the worship began. Suddenly an older man rushed up to the front and started dancing, whirling around with his arms flailing. He looked like a topsy-turvy helicopter about to lift off. There was no sense of rhythm; it was just pure, random movement. But he was lost in the moment.

"Now that's distracting," I thought, but I tried not to dwell on it. Who was I to judge? The man kept it up for a couple songs, then went back to his seat, and no one else seemed to mind or even notice! I chalked it up to an eccentric saint who needed dance lessons.

Several months later, I happened to speak at the same church again. And once more, when the worship started, the man came to the front and started his exuberant worship expression. I had actually forgotten about my previous experience. This time I could feel my heart instantly begin to judge him, and I wondered why an usher didn't come to deal with him. There was no reason to allow such strange behavior that distracted others from the worship time. Strangely enough, I seemed to be the only one who noticed!

After service, the associate pastor and I went out to lunch. I decided this was my opportunity to speak up about my dancing friend.

"What's the story with that guy who comes flying out of the crowd and dances at worship?" I asked, an edge to my voice.

He thought for a minute, actually trying to figure out who I was talking about! Then he said, "Oh that guy, yeah, that's a wild story," the pastor said. "That brother had been paralyzed in a wheelchair for seven years after a car accident; and in a prayer service about six months ago, God healed him miraculously. He stood up out of his chair that night on his own power; and ever since then, we can't get him to stop dancing."

We can't get him to stop dancing. "Wow, that's amazing!" I said, but internally I was so disappointed in myself. I had been completely uninformed and missed seeing what life looked like from his perspective. I judged him, and my hard heart could not share his joy. If God had pulled me out of a wheelchair, I'd be dancing, too.

Stop to think with me now. Have you ever been sincerely convinced that you were right about something only to discover later you were wrong when new information was revealed? I don't think this is just me. We all have, right? Sincerity is celebrated in our culture as the be-all, end-all of every opinion. In fact, sincerity can be used to justify a lot of awful behavior. Now sincerity is a wonderful virtue in most cases, but you can be sincere and still be dead wrong about something.

In that moment, wisdom and humility would ask me, "In what other areas might I be sincerely wrong about someone or something simply because there is information I do not yet have or understand?"

How often do we dig in our heels about something, remaining in ignorance, instead of being willing to see things differently? Wisdom is able to step back and see things in the larger context. My ignorance kept me from discerning that the man wasn't a distraction but was in fact a living testimony of God's healing power to everyone in that church every Sunday that he danced. Everyone knew it but me. Ouch.

Choosing the Ancient Path

Each year, the tech industry has an event to excitedly announce whatever shiny, new things they are offering that year: new colors, faster memory, improved camera, exciting AI—all to be forgotten as old and outdated in just a short time.

God told a stubborn group of Israelites that, when they stood at the crossroads, they were to ask for the ancient path (Jeremiah 6:16). "Stand there for a moment, and look," He said. "Ask for the ancient path. Ask where the good way is and then walk in it. That's where you'll find rest for your souls."

But the Israelites said they would not walk that way. So, they and their families ate the fruit of their decisions. The human condition is timeless. The ancient path never becomes outdated. But today we are taught to value what's new, not what's old.

"New is better!" is the cry of today's entrepreneur. If you think about it, "new" things aren't truly new. They simply unfolded from God's hand just now.

A cutting-edge ruler of the ancient world once wrote "there is nothing new under the sun" (Ecclesiastes 1:9). These words were written in the fourth quarter of a life filled with the accumulation of knowledge and experiences. Kings and queens came from the ends of the earth to see the riches of Solomon and to hear his wisdom. What are we to make of that? We are enticed with the idea that the "new" thing is always the better thing. Think about the iPhone. To younger generations, it might feel as if the world has used smartphones forever. Immediate access to a world of knowledge is just how people have always lived. But it hasn't been. Smartphones are a relatively new type of technology, one that in recent years has started to raise concerns.

It's a common movie trope to have a character that serves as a guide who knows what's behind the curtain. Gandalf in *Lord of the Rings*, for example, knows what's going on and tries to guide the fellowship in completing their mission to destroy the ring, even though the members of the fellowship aren't quite sure what's really happening and why. A big part of their success is sticking with what the sage told them needed to be done—whether or not it made sense at the time.

Stubbornness resists the ancient ways.

When we're stubborn and stand at the crossroads of decision, we often tend to repeat painful, foolish history instead of acknowledging that God may have a better way. "This time it will be different," we tell ourselves. It seldom is. History has a way of repeating itself, and a wise person will be a student of their history.

There is nothing new under the sun, but there are new distractions that play into the same old cravings of the heart. They are just repackaged for our current situation. They are the clickbait of a wandering soul. The ancient paths of our Creator are the only sure, dependable way to live well. He alone is qualified to walk you through a life that works.

Have you considered the splinters you have and where you got them?

Are you willing to recognize what you don't know?

Are you resisting the ancient path in favor of always chasing something new that promises, but never delivers?

What would be driving this?

Asking why we do what we do isn't morbid self-introspection. It is wise to consider what has shaped our lives, to try to understand ourselves, and to consider that the people around us have their own stories, too.

The Pain That Holds Us Back

Years ago, a young woman on my staff began to struggle. It seemed to come out of nowhere. She was an incredibly talented, beautiful, and brilliant person, gifted in just about everything she laid her hands on. Her musical ability was especially impressive, but she was also skilled as an administrator because she was kind and highly organized. Everything about her was an A-plus.

But after several years of working at the church, she began to have horrific nightmares. Her life started to fall apart, and none of it made any sense. From what we could tell, she was a stable and godly young woman.

Agreeing to go to counseling, the experienced therapist helped her open a door to her past she'd never allowed to be opened. Behind that door hid terrible memories of abuse at the hands of a family member who worked at a large church. A young child who is abused like that has no understanding of what is happening or how to interpret it. What's worse, she was threatened to tell no one or her family would be destroyed.

She became convinced that she was alone in life and had to protect herself. No one could ever know her horrible secret, including her family. Talking to the people she loved the most would bring them ruin.

For a while, that instinct protected her. She avoided her father; and when she was invited to go camping or spend the night with friends, she chose not to because she'd be alone and vulnerable. She knew there were bad people out there.

But the protection that trauma-based instincts provide only serves us for a season.

Twenty years later, her life was very different. She was thriving in a Christian college and in ministry at church. She met a wonderful Christian man who would love to marry her; and while she was attracted to him, her self-protection instinct kept her from giving him any signals that she was interested. One evening, while they were studying together in the school library, he reached over innocently to squeeze her hand. She quickly got up and left, leaving him confused. The instincts that had kept her alive since she was a child were now crushing her life as an adult. What had served her well was now working against her.

Pete Scazzaro has written extensively about this in his books on emotionally healthy living. In *Emotionally Healthy Churches*, he says: "In emotionally healthy churches people understand how their past affects their present ability to love Christ and others … they've realized from scripture and life that an intricate, complex relationship exists between the kind of person they are today and their past. Numerous external forces may shape us but the family we have grown up in is the primary and, except in rare instances, the most powerful system that will change and influence who we are."

Think of the child who grew up homeless or in instability in the foster care system who hoards food as an adult, remembering what it was like to grow up not having enough to eat. Think of the man berated by his parents for failures and imperfections, growing up to become a hard, performance-driven person who tolerates nothing but success in the people around him. Think of the young woman ostracized by her peers or told that she was unlovable who then goes on to become a high-functioning adult perfectionist who will do whatever it takes to prove she has value.

These wounds have shaped us. And sometimes we find ourselves speaking and living through those wounds. Over my years of counseling people, I've noticed that what comes out as the problem is mostly just what's on the surface. People tell me why they're fighting, why they're unhappy, what is wrong; and yet I can feel an undercurrent of something else driving the conflict.

What is really behind how people behave? Why are they so driven? Self-sufficient to the point of refusing any help? Disgusted by failure? Promiscuous? Hard and accusatory? Unwilling to help? What do they really fear?

The real problem remains invisible while we frantically put bandages on the surface problems. We hoping to find a fix, frantically have to go deeper to find the source: the trauma that might lurk deep that's driving so much more than we realize. As fellow travelers, we must walk very carefully here because the healing of those wounds is holy ground to God.

Identify The Lie

The human spirit can endure a sick body,
but who can bear a crushed spirit?
Proverbs 18:14 (NLT)

That young woman who had been abused and whose life was starting to fall apart ended up finding her way out to freedom. It wasn't easy, but a large part of her success was recognizing what had taken place. A wicked man had taken advantage of a vulnerable girl, and then on top of that, he burdened her with shame and the guilt of it all. *If you tell your dad, you'll ruin your family.*

It wasn't true, but that simple lie had spawned endless patterns in her life. She had to go through each pattern that the lie had produced, identify it for what it was, and replace it with truth. The truth according to a loving heavenly Father. This is actually the working definition of true repentance as well as the road to freedom. I allow God to change my mind about something, and in turn that begins to reshape my behavior. The hiding, the self-sufficiency, the secrets—they all stemmed from deception, and it was crushing her life. I am in no way suggesting that childhood trauma is easily solved by simply disagreeing with the lies involved in what happened. But truth is the rock that I can stand on when all else fails me. This is why Jesus said, "The thief comes only to steal and kill and destroy. I came that they may have life and have it abundantly" (John 10:10). Her amazing journey of healing held fast because the Wonderful Counselor, Mighty God, and Prince of Peace proved Himself faithful and trustworthy to her. It often seems easy as an outside observer to look into the windows of someone's life and see what's inside, but is our observation accurate? Am I seeing my life through a clear lens?

My father grew up during the Great Depression and served in World War II flying combat missions in the South Pacific. There was a lot of his life he never talked about, and I could never have understood even if he did. When I was a young person, we would work on home projects together. He would have me unbend the used nails when we were finished in order to use them again. It seemed like such a pointless thing, and it wasn't until years later that I began to realize why.

The Great Depression world my dad grew up in was very different from my own, where nails are now plentiful and cheap. It was easy to see the fear of scarcity mentality at work in my father's life. But what we miss when we look in someone else's window is our own reflection staring back. We have to refocus and identify the untruths operating in our own lives.

Live in the Present Reality

For my dad, nothing was ever wasted. You didn't throw away a bad nail because you might find use for it later. You used every rivet. You couldn't get enough gas. There were ration books for staple foods. You grew victory gardens. You saved all the metal for the war effort. From children to adults, this was their way of life. It's what was called a wartime mentality. The battle wasn't just overseas; it affected every aspect of their existence.

That mentality affected entire generations and didn't end just because the war did. It stuck around for decades after, affecting even the generations who didn't live through it.

The young woman who was abused was living in the past, even though her present reality was much different. In the school library, instead of enjoying the attention of the young man, she reverted to thinking he would hurt her. That was a wartime mentality, too. She thought she was at war with that young man, even though the war had been with her uncle many years earlier.

The mechanisms of the past don't always serve us well in the present.

WISDOM IS CONSTANT COURSE CORRECTION

It was a new moon, and the overcast skies clouded any light that the stars could give. In the inky darkness, a large navy vessel spotted a light in the distance. Assuming another ship was out on the water with them, the navy vessel established radio contact but proceeded on course.

"Please divert your course twenty degrees south to avoid a collision," the naval vessel radioed.

There was a pause, and then the radio crackled. "Recommend you divert twenty degrees north to avoid collision."

Back and forth the two went, strenuously recommending that the other divert course. Finally, the naval ship had had enough. "We are a battleship," they radioed. "Divert course or measures will be taken to ensure the safety of this ship."

Another pause before the second voice responded. "This is a lighthouse. Your call."

It's a classic story; whether it's true or not doesn't matter as much as recognizing that stubbornness doesn't serve us well when it comes to course correction. Being willing to change course is necessary if you want a life that works.

Imagine that we symbolized a life that works as living our dream life in Hawaii: beautiful sunsets, warm breezes, sandy beaches, and all the tropical fruits you could eat. To get there requires a long journey in your sailboat. You know the location of Hawaii, which is good; but if you don't understand drift and the dangers it brings, you're naive and unlikely to make it.

Stubbornly insisting that Hawaii was west of where you started and holding to that same course, ignoring wind and ocean currents, may land you on a deserted island somewhere far from Hawaii.

Wisdom is dynamic, not static. Unlike mathematics, which deals in absolutes, wisdom requires us to be attuned to subtle changes and shifting contexts. This means that everyday life demands constant fine-tuning. It's like sailing: we must continually check the wind and currents, adjust our sails, and verify our position—it's an ongoing application of knowledge, not just the collection of it.

For pilots, winds can easily push them off course, even if it seems like the nose of the airplane is pointed in the right direction. A pilot has to keep their eyes ahead, trusting his instruments, making sure that the destination direction stays front and center, even if the nose of the aircraft is at an angle to compensate for winds.

What's tricky about course correction, whether on water or in the air, is that overcorrecting in the opposite direction only puts you on course for a moment. Then you're off course in the opposite direction, still no more likely to reach your destination than before.

Wisdom is constant, steady course correction.

And because wisdom is so dynamic, it defies formula.

What worked well in one situation might not in another. Situations are unique, and people don't always respond the same way. A stubborn person often finds the lack of a predictable formula troubling.

Wisdom defying a formula is one of the reasons why people who try to make the book of Proverbs into something formulaic run into problems. They get frustrated, because things don't systematically work out the same every time.

Some things are, and will be, mysterious and without explanation.

For those who like a formula, this dynamic nature is going to seem like God failing them. It's easy to think that, if God won't uphold His end of the bargain (i.e. the formula we think is at work), then we can go our own way. This is the difference between a transactional and a transformational relationship. God reveals Himself to be a friend who is in this with us for the long haul, always working the myriads of life's circumstances for His ultimate glory and for our eternal best interests.

WISDOM REQUIRES DISCERNMENT

I had a friend who worked at a well-known camping store located in a mountain climbing area of the country. People would come into the store and tell him they wanted to buy some crampons, backpacks, hiking sticks—all the gear you'd need to climb the mountain.

But my friend would often wonder if they knew what they were doing. Nothing about them, either in appearance or in how they talked about the gear, indicated they had mountain climbing experience.

"What do you have planned?" my friend would ask them.

"We're going to climb Mt. Shasta," might be the response.

"When are you going to do it?" he'd ask.

"We were thinking about going this weekend. Do you have any advice?"

And then my friend would proceed to tell them "Yes, don't do it!" He thought it was a bad plan because they had no idea what they were doing. Being able to buy the gear doesn't guarantee success. They thought it was just a simple hike, but my friend knew better. His job was to sell gear, but he also didn't want people to get hurt. Not everyone took his advice, though, because people are like that. They don't know what they don't understand.

They want to sail to Hawaii, climb to the mountaintop or have a life that works; but they don't want the inconvenience of admitting they need to change course and put in the work that would make them better prepared for what's ahead. They aren't discerning what's necessary and instead leave things up to chance.

The Stages of Immaturity

There is an idea that human beings exist in three stages of immaturity.

The first is an immaturity of knowledge, which is often marked by a lack of life experience. You simply haven't lived long enough to know all you need to know. But as a child or young person, the freedom to do very much is limited; so there's a measure of protection. You're in a safe place, but you don't stay there long because there is a big world out there waiting to be discovered.

The second stage is the immaturity of wisdom. You're older, you're physically more mature, and you find yourself at the crossroads of freedom and experience. It can be an exciting yet vulnerable place of trying out untested ideas to see how they will work in real life. It's here that it begins to dawn on you the number of things that you don't know. That understanding is actually very healthy.

The third immaturity is one of discipline. At this stage, we have knowledge, opportunity, and freedom to do what we want. We may have accumulated some measure of power and resources. But we can squander it all by a lack of discipline. And for most of us, discipline does not come easy (Proverbs 5:12). Just look around at how many leads have been squandered in the final quarter or races won or lost down at the finish line. What good is running a strong race if we do not finish well?

> BEING DILIGENT MEANS TO BE IN A PERSISTENT STATE OF AIMING TO ACCOMPLISH SOMETHING. IT'S BEING CONSISTENT IN HOW YOU CONDUCT YOUR LIFE, ALIGNING EVERYTHING YOU DO WITH THE KIND OF OUTCOME YOU DESIRE. IN THIS CASE, THAT OUTCOME IS A LIFE THAT WORKS.

A Time for Due Diligence

Being diligent means to be in a persistent state of aiming to accomplish something. It's being consistent in how you conduct your life, aligning everything you do with the kind of outcome you desire. In this case, that outcome is a life that works.

That means diligence in our relationships, in how we manage our resources, and in the daily decisions we make about what we consume and the words we speak. It also means we have to have the right priorities.

The world tells us to be diligent, too, but not in the same way.

A rich farmer, whose grain bins were overflowing with wheat, realized he had no place to store the crops from the current year. Harvest was coming soon, and he'd need somewhere to store it.

"I'll have to tear down my small bins and build much bigger ones," he said. "I can store the extra grain that way, and I'll have so much grain stored away that I should be able to retire and take life easy."

Too bad he didn't know he was going to die that night (Luke 12:16–21).

The farmer was diligent, but he wasn't aligned with God's values.

Discernment Doesn't Function by Chance

Israel was at war, but King David wasn't living as if that was the reality (2 Samuel 11). Instead of being on the battleship, he was on the cruise ship. While his men were on the front lines, he was back at the palace.

That's when he saw Bathsheba.

It's almost as if he thought seeing her was his reward for all of his hard work and kingly excellence. Surely it wasn't by chance that he happened to be at the palace, at that window, at the moment when a beautiful woman was bathing. His choices then set in motion the downfall that led to adultery, murder, and an infant's death, not to mention the wreckage in his own family for future generations.

Many a reader has wondered how David, a man after God's own heart, could do such a foolhardy thing.

But we have more in common with David than we like to admit.

"This must be a God moment!" I hear so often from people when they're about to do something they will later regret. They justify it, saying that all of the circumstances that lead to the moment surely can't be an accident. It's as if they have no choice but to take action. Fate had dictated their path. When everything lines up like that, someone has to bring Bathsheba to the palace. And we know that is not where the story ended.

Like David did, it's easy to tell ourselves in a place of self-indulgence that nothing bad has happened as a result of a poor choice. So, how could I be wrong? A critical mistake we make here is that we confuse God's mercy with God's permission.

It may be that the signs along our path aren't signs but wreckage. We can make a choice in those moments. For many years, I have found myself often asking people, "What was going through your mind when you made that decision? Where was God in that moment?"

A.W. Tozer once compared the thorny question of man's free will to a cruise ship. God, in His sovereign power and will, says that the ship will leave New York and arrive in London on a specific date and time. The passengers don't know the date; but regardless, no human intervention will stop that ship from arriving when God has determined it will. All the passengers know is that they'll get on the ship in New York and that when they arrive in London, the cruise is over.

The passengers' free will, however, means they can make that trip an enjoyable one; or it can be hell on earth. Each person on that ship will act as they choose, and their choices will have significance for everyone onboard.

It's true. We will one day come to the end of our life. We can walk in discernment and wisdom, or we can leave it up to chance. We can wait until moments come together and let outside events dictate our course in life, or we can choose God's wise counsel.

David knew better. By the end of his life, he had learned. As he was dying, he had one last thing to say to his son Solomon (1 Kings 2:1–4).

"I'm about to die," he said. "Be strong. Observe what God requires. Walk in obedience to him and keep his commands. If you do this, you'll prosper in all that you do and wherever you go."

Shalom is the Biblical concept of peace, prosperity, harmony, and righteousness in every area of life.

What David wanted for his son, more than anything, was a life of *shalom*.

CHAPTER SIX REFLECTIONS:
CORRECTION, CONVERSION, AND HEALING

1) What course corrections have I made in my life that have saved me from grief? Were those corrections easy or difficult, and why?

2) Can I think of an example where God had to change my mind about something before I could really change my behavior? How did that work, and why was that important?

3) Are there areas of my life where I see patterns that might be driven by unseen currents of my past? How could I invite Jesus into those areas and allow Him to begin the healing process in me? How might forgiveness toward another or understanding truth play a part in that process?

CHAPTER SEVEN

Watch Your Mouth

*"We have two ears and one mouth so that
we can listen twice as much as we speak."*
– Epictetus

*"The words of the reckless pierce like swords,
but the tongue of the wise brings healing."*
– Proverbs 12:18 (NIV)

It had almost become a game for the boy, saying awful things to his sister. He made fun of how she looked, what she said, what she did—anything that would make her cry. He became a master at using words to cut; and even though his parents would make him apologize to her, he'd start up again in a few days.

"Son," his dad said to him one Saturday morning, "I need your help building a little fence in the backyard for the dog."

The boy helped his dad gather the wood and the nails, and soon they were busy hammering together a fence. Hours later, tired from the work, the boy thought they were done. Looking forward to a cold glass of lemonade, he started towards the house.

"We're not done," his dad said. "I want you to help me take this fence apart, board by board, and move it."

This was going to take more time than building the fence! The boy was upset, wondering why he was being punished. Pulling the first board off the frame, he was about to toss it in a pile and move to the second board when his dad stopped him.

~

OUR WORDS HAVE THE POWER TO ENCOURAGE LIFE AND/OR CREATE GREAT DAMAGE, NOT ONLY IN THE PERSON WE SAY THEM TO, BUT ALSO IN OUR OWN BODY AND SPIRIT.

~

"I want you to take each nail out of the board."

Grumbling under his breath, the boy flipped his hammer over and wedged the nail free from the board.

"Now make that nail hole go away," the dad said.

The boy didn't know whether to laugh or cry. Removing the nail was one thing, but removing the hole it left behind? It couldn't be done.

Pointing to the hole in the board, his dad spoke quietly. "That hole in the board is like your words. You can't take them back. You can say you're sorry, but the damage is already done."

Our words have the power to encourage life and/or create great damage, not only in the person we say them to, but also in our own body and spirit.

WORDS CAN BRING LIFE OR DEATH

Sticks and stones may break my bones, but words will never hurt me. We know that's a lie because we all carry the scars of words that have hurt us.

You can heal from wounds caused by sticks and stones. A good doctor or antiseptic and bandage will do the trick. But words used carelessly wound much deeper and for longer. Words can bring healing, or they can be weapons (Proverbs 15:4); and it's not just the person on the receiving end of those words who can be built up or torn down. God tells us that our soul is nourished when we're kind, but it's destroyed when we are cruel (Proverbs 11:17).

I once had a defining moment in my life but didn't even realize it at the time. I was about sixteen and playing sports in high school. My coach was an old-school type who would ride us without mercy. Looking back now, he was downright abusive in the way he treated his players; but when you're the kid and he is the authority figure, it's difficult to see.

One afternoon I did something wrong, and he whistled the play dead and then screamed at me from across the field. The play resumed, I repeated my mistake, and again came the verbal correction. When it happened the third time, he went to another level. He was so mad that he ran over to me, grabbed my jersey, and screamed at me, "Stefanik, you should just quit playing this game because you're too f*****g stupid to play it!" I could feel the heat of his anger and my own deep shame as my teammates watched helplessly. I was not a follower of Jesus at the time; so under my breath, I cursed him back and took his advice and quit that team.

I didn't think much of it for the next twenty years. Then one day I was working in another country, leading a team in a full-time ministry. I had hit a wall and was at a loss as to what to do next. It was so bad that I took the day off and went out to a nearby lake by myself to have a time of prayer and a pity party. As I sat there on the dock that afternoon, I remember telling God my exit strategy. I was going to head back home and do something more respectable with less headache. I asked if He would please bless my idea. I was going to quit on my calling. Then it was like a video began to play in my mind of that event that had taken place two decades earlier. I saw it in living color replayed with all the details. That fall day on the field, my teammates, that screaming coach and worst of all my private pain that I'd never talked to anyone about. Then I heard God speak to me as clearly as I have ever heard Him. He said, "Bruce, you need to repent of what happened that day." My response was, "Why do I need to repent? He was the authority figure who should have known better! He was the one who spoke those words over me!" and God gently said, "Son, he said it, but you believed it!" It shocked me because I realized that a flawed human being had spoken a reckless lie over my life that I was too stupid to play, and I had received it as truth. It had shaped the way I saw myself and told me quitting was the answer. I realized at that moment that not every word brings life, and some are meant for death.

Are you stressed? Angry? Frantically refreshing your phone to see what idiot responded to you on social media and preparing your response? Then this might be a good time to tell you that speaking kind words has a healing effect on your body. They are like honey, sweet to the spirit (Proverbs 16:24). It makes sense, if you think about it. Unkind words are a poison; and when they become the language we are most fluent in, it's not just the people around us who suffer. We do, as well, and even our bodies aren't left unscathed. It's the things that come out of our mouth that contaminate us. All of the evil thoughts, the hate, the immorality, the theft and slander and lies—when we speak them, we give them life by putting them into ears and hearts around us (including our own).

Words are not our enemy. They are powerful when used the right way. It's how we communicate information, how we express heartfelt emotion and share ideas. Words convey a lot, making us feel loved (or hated). They can bless (or curse). They can share the truth (or a lie). They can encourage or discourage. Think about those two words. How many times have positive or affirming words given you strength for what you were facing? When someone comes alongside you and says, "*I believe in you, you can do this,*" or "*I am here for you,*" how do you feel? You feel empowered and energized. You realize that you are no longer alone. In that moment, that person sees you and literally "gives you courage" for whatever it is you are facing. I once had a gentleman come up to me and tell me he had a prophetic gift to see what's wrong in the church. I thought to myself, "now that is a cheap and common gift, if it is a gift at all!" Anybody can see what's wrong in a church or a person if they just observe long enough. Only seeing what is wrong with the world is what feeds the beast of the 24/7 news machine. I want to be the kind of person who can see what is good or praiseworthy in a person. I want to call out the best in them, not the worst. I don't want to be a taker but a giver of life with what comes out of my mouth.

"Words are just words" is a dangerous game to play. Even our legal system recognizes that words carry some level of power. If you lie in a court of law or in business or in a contract, you'll be held accountable. And if words were nothing, there would be no such thing as phone sex. We all know that words have the power to move us, change us, motivate us, or cause us to become numb.

God is all about words. He is very verbal, and His son Jesus Christ is known as The Word (John 1:1). He can communicate better than anyone or anything in the universe, and He has used words over the ages to communicate with us. He has woven intricate tapestries in His Word, with passages leaping off the page in a new way each time we read them.

In a way, it's frustrating to hear people say that they can't hear from God because what He does with us is communicate. His creation speaks out, His Word is alive and active, His teachers and pastors speak to us, His Spirit helps us— suggesting that the Creator of the universe can't figure out how to communicate with us is a stretch. Often when people say to me they can't hear God's voice, I suggest they try reading His Word out loud!

As image bearers of God, we can do a lot with our words.

It's no small wonder that so many of the passages in the book of Proverbs focus on controlling our tongue and being careful about what comes out of our mouth.

It's not only that we can do damage to others and ourselves with careless words, but also that our words reflect what's happening in our heart.

Your Words Reveal What's Inside

Jesus said what's in our heart is what comes out of our mouth (Matthew 12:34). Our words and how we use them are a dead giveaway for what's in our heart, no matter how well we've tried to disguise it.

I'm always amazed by the things that come out of people's mouths. It's almost as if they have no filter whatsoever. It's even worse online, particularly on social media. People will say just about anything online. They'll say things to or about people they'd never say in person.

What's even more scary, in those moments, is I realize what's in their heart.

Someone goes off, horrible words come out, and I call them on it.

"Well, it's just because I'm an angry type of person," they respond, as if anger creates the words out of thin air. Others will argue it's just their genetics, as if one ethnicity tends to anger more than another.

They might be angry, but all that serves as is a pressure valve, popping the top off of what's bottled up inside. The words were already there, waiting for an opportunity.

Paul writes that we shouldn't let any corrupt communication come out of our mouth, but only what is useful for building others up according to the need, so it can benefit those who listen. He then tells us we should not grieve the Holy Spirit of God (Ephesians 4:29–30).

But there's more to it.

Paying attention to the words coming out of our mouth is important for another reason: it's an early indicator of an anger problem.

Get rid of all bitterness, rage and anger, brawling and slander, along with every form of malice, Paul writes next (Ephesians 4:31), connecting the dots between our words and anger. One of the ways of stopping the words that come out in anger is forgiveness, something we'll cover more in the next chapter. But before we get there, we have to understand the price of what comes out of our mouth.

Every Word Will Be Accounted For

By the time this section is done, you may feel like deleting your social media accounts, or at least taking a hiatus. Because after pointing out that our words reveal what's in our heart, Jesus went on to say that on the day of judgment, every single one of us would give an account of every careless word we said, and that by our words we'd either be acquitted or condemned (Matthew 12:36–37).

How many careless words have we said over the years?

Do you rush into quarrels that aren't yours to fight about? You're like a person who grabs an angry, mad dog by the ears (Proverbs 26:17). Could Solomon have seen social media coming when he wrote this? If tempers are flaring around you, do you rush to join the fray? Do you respond in a gentle way to lessen the heat, or in a witty, cutting manner to make people all the angrier (Proverbs 15:1)? Bet you didn't know that God was paying attention like that. Did you realize He was following you on Facebook? On X?

A friend of mine got a traffic ticket that he decided to take to court instead of just mailing in a check. He described the experience as an opportunity to meet really "interesting" people. What struck him the most, however, was how people behaved in front of the judge.

They were there to fight.

"I didn't do this!" they would say, insisting that their ticket was undeserved.

One man approached the bench and laid out his claim with an appeal to experience. "I've been driving that road for fifteen years, and they just changed that speed limit."

"I've been a judge for twenty years, and that speed limit has been the same the entire time," the judge said.

As he waited my friend felt his confidence levels dropping to critical, unsure of how to protest the ticket knowing the judge would respond with plain truth.

But not everyone approached the judge to argue their innocence. Some would admit they'd done wrong and say they were sorry. The difference between those who approached the bench with pride, hoping to fight the law and win, were hit with that same law. The judge made it clear they had to pay their fine and leave. Those who were sincerely apologetic received more leniency. They still had to pay a fine, but it was significantly reduced.

When my friend approached the bench, he chose the latter way.

"I'm sorry. I guess I plead guilty," he said to the judge, who ended up reducing his fine.

Now consider the day we stand before a Judge and have to give an account for the words that came out of our mouth. Will we try to justify and defend what we've said? Are our words even defensible? Or will we acknowledge our fault, our sin, humbly plead guilty, and let Jesus's blood cover it?

This should be a very sobering thought.

> ❧
>
> **WHAT JESUS DID ON THE CROSS WAS A HIGH PRICE TO PAY FOR YOU TO SIMPLY ARGUE ABOUT POLITICS WITH SOMEONE ON FACEBOOK.**
>
> ❧

What Jesus did on the cross was a high price to pay for you to simply argue about politics with someone on Facebook.

TRUTHFULNESS IN WHAT WE SPEAK

God hates the very lips that tell lies, but He is delighted in people who are trustworthy (Proverbs 12:22). God cares about the truth. It's important to Him.

But truth is valued less and less in our culture. We place a premium on feelings or what the words can get people to do. We use words to be provocative, to catch attention, to spark emotions, to move the needle in the direction we prefer. We end up with politicians who will say anything to get a vote. We have influencers who will promote anything for money. We have corporations who will say whatever agrees with what's trending. There is almost no accountability when a lie is exposed. It's almost as if lying is so normalized that we not only expect it but excuse it.

What does it mean to be a person of integrity? Do you want your friends, your spouse, or your business partner to be someone who lies, a person who can't be trusted? We all want to surround ourselves with people who are honest with us.

Proverbs 13 says that from the fruit of our lips people enjoy good things, but the unfaithful have an appetite for violence. Whoever guards his mouth preserves his life, but those who speak carelessly will be destroyed. The righteous hate what is false and guard the person of integrity.

Honesty and integrity go hand in hand.

Integrity is adhering to moral and ethical principles, having a sound character in which our entire being is undiminished. Think about an ocean-going ship, crossing the Atlantic. If the hull doesn't have integrity, water gets inside and the ship sinks. In the same way, if we don't have integrity something else gets inside and pulls us down.

We don't ride on ships without hull integrity. We certainly wouldn't knowingly board an airplane without wing integrity. We wouldn't drive across a bridge that didn't have structural integrity.

When a person loses integrity, lives around them are destroyed. As more people lose integrity, a community is destroyed. And as communities of people lose integrity, nations are destroyed.

A friend of mine who lived in China watched the Three Gorges Dam construction. This is the largest dam in the world, spanning the Yangtze River in Hubei province, China. The structure is almost impossible to comprehend.

But someone without integrity was allowed to work on the construction and they happily took the money while using inferior cement. It worked out well for them, charging for high quality and delivering something much cheaper. But it resulted in part of the dam they'd built being torn out at great expense to the nation. Weak cement in a dam leads to catastrophe and lost lives, especially in a dam as big as Three Gorges.

China took the situation so seriously that those who tried to cheat on the project received the death sentence.

We tell a lie, and our integrity starts taking a hit. Things seem fine for a while, but something's going to break. It's going to take us (and those around us) down.

So, how do we cut down on lying?

Speak Less, Pray More

In an incessantly noisy world, silence is loud.

Proverbs 21:23 tells us that whoever guards their mouth and tongue keeps themself from calamity.

In the 1994 movie *Forrest Gump*, one of the iconic scenes is of Forrest running back and forth across the country. He had proposed to Jenny, the love of his life, and was rejected.

As a child, cornered by bullies, Jenny had helped him escape with one simple message: Run, Forrest, run!

And that's what he did. Running had helped him make it through college and the Vietnam War, and it seemed like the right thing to do.

"That day, for no particular reason, I decided to go for a little run," he explained to the woman on the bench. Forrest ran from his home in Alabama out to the California coast and then turned around and ran to the Atlantic coast. He crossed the Mississippi River four times, and people pressed him to tell them why he was running. They wanted him to speak up and put words out there so they could understand (or maybe get a sound bite). His story caught the attention of the press wherever he traveled, and people were inspired to run with him. They had all kinds of reasons to run and would tell him so.

But he never said much in over three years of running. And somewhere in Utah's Monument Valley, he slowed to a stop. The crowd that had been following him stopped too, whispering in hushed tones. Forrest turned around and faced the crowd.

"Quiet! Quiet! He's going to say something!"

There was a long pause, and he finally spoke up. "I'm pretty tired. I think I'll go home now."

What a mic drop moment.

Forrest Gump is just a fictional movie, but would he have accomplished his run if he had spent his time speaking? Would he have inspired people if he'd vented all the time on any and everything? Would he have had clarity of mind and purpose if he'd lashed out, gossiped, or slandered people along the way?

In an age of information and influencers, we're under a constant bombardment of words. Every moment, every tragedy, every news event, every concert, every vacation—if there's a mic in the room, someone will fill the air with words.

We need to say less and pray more.

Be quick to listen, not speak. Being slow to speak is connected to being slow to becoming angry (James 1:19). It's not easy; but with practice, we can starve the part of ourselves that wants to lash out immediately and keep the anger going. We can be angry but not commit sin along with it by choosing to be silent and think (Psalms 4:4).

Take that frustration, or that witty and sarcastic comeback, to God instead of hammering another volley of words into someone's spirit that you can't take back even if you're sorry those words escaped your mouth. It's easier to gossip about someone instead of praying for them.

Practice waiting a few minutes or an hour or a day or even a week before hitting publish or responding to someone who happened to find just the right button of yours to push. It's thought that Thomas Jefferson once said, "If we're angry, we should count to ten before we speak; if we're very angry, we should count to one hundred."

Consider if the things you want to say or share are self-centered or uplifting of others. We're addicted to looking at our own faces and to the sound of our own voices.

Never has a generation had more ability to say what's on their mind, more venues to speak, and so little to say. We are drowning in an ocean of comparisons and opinions. Much of it is belittling others and pushing them down to raise yourself up.

The upside to speaking less? Even a fool is thought to be wise and discerning if they close their mouth and hold their tongue! (Proverbs 17:28). Wait, did I hear that right? I will be perceived as wise if I simply listen more and talk less? We have all been in meetings or conversations where the opposite kind of person is present. A fool takes no pleasure in understanding, but only in expressing his opinion (Proverbs 18:2). Stop and ask yourself at that moment, "Do I feel more valued or less? More heard and seen or more invisible?"

We have to communicate. Our only two options aren't simply speak up and say something we'll regret, or stuff it down inside and grow bitter. There is another option. If more of our words were directed to God in prayer, our hearts will reflect that; and so will our mouth. Why wouldn't we take all our cares and frustrations and concerns to the One who can do something about them anyway? God is the only one who can make a difference.

Speak less and pray more so that, in the end, you ultimately say more.

Make Right Your Lies

Tell a lie, and soon you'll have to tell another. This continues until you're backed into a corner or until you stop the pattern. Sin isn't ended by saying more, but by holding our tongue (Proverbs 10:19). And then we make right what we've lied about.

One of the best deterrents to lying is realizing that you'll have to go back to make it right. It's an especially great deterrent if you're struggling with the fear of man because that's the fear that gets to the heart of lying.

We're afraid of what someone might think.

Most of the time, when we're struggling to tell the truth, it's because we want someone to think better of us or want to avoid getting into trouble.

When we get in the habit of going back to tell the truth to someone after we've told a lie, we'll start speaking less. We know that the words that leave our mouth have follow-up, and it's up to us to determine how painful and messy that will be.

> WE KNOW THAT THE WORDS THAT LEAVE OUR MOUTH HAVE FOLLOW-UP, AND IT'S UP TO US TO DETERMINE HOW PAINFUL AND MESSY THAT WILL BE.

Even better than avoiding lying because of the pain of making it right is the accountability you build with your closest community. Confessing our lies to someone makes it possible for them to pray for us (James 5:16). Building a community of accountability is building a community of honesty.

"A word fitly spoken is like apples of gold in a setting of silver. Like a gold ring or an ornament of gold is a wise reprover to a listening ear" (Proverbs 25:10–12 ESV).

Honesty can be painful at times. There are people who, wanting to avoid the hurt that might come with being honest and unwilling to test a relationship, will never speak the direct truth, even when we need it spoken to us in love.

CHAPTER SEVEN REFLECTIONS:
WOUNDS, WISDOM, AND WELLNESS

1) Think back for a moment to your past. Are there words that were spoken to you or over you that have done damage to your heart? Perhaps they have stolen your courage or distorted your identity? As you bring them to mind, ask the Father what He has to say about what happened. More importantly, what would He say about you now?

2) What kind of words bring healing and courage to your soul? Who do you have around you that would benefit from a "courage-giving" word?

3) What does "setting a guard at my mouth" mean in my life? How often do I find exaggeration, criticism, or sarcasm coming out of my mouth?

4) What would change if I set a goal of just speaking one encouraging word a day to someone?

CHAPTER EIGHT

Anger and Compassion

"How much more grievous are the consequences
of anger than the causes of it."
– Marcus Aurelius

"For as churning cream produces butter,
and as twisting the nose produces blood,
so stirring up anger produces strife."
– Proverbs 30:33 (NIV)

"Whoever is slow to anger is better
than the mighty, and he who rules his
spirit than he who takes a city."
– Proverbs 16:32 (ESV)

As a farmer, Cain probably wished the ground would stop screaming.

Both he and his brother, Abel, had presented their first fruits to God. Abel's was of his flock; Cain's was from his fields. But something about how Cain had done it hadn't pleased God, and Cain became angry when his offering wasn't accepted. He sulked and then he plotted. And in his anger, he took his brother out to his field and murdered him.

God told Cain he was cursed, and the ground he worked as a farmer had swallowed up Abel's blood and cried out because of it.

By the time we get to Jesus, murder had changed a bit.

We no longer have to take someone out to the middle of nowhere and do them in. Now, just having hate in our heart is as good as murdering someone. Think of how hate-filled and angry our current culture is and multiply that across history. There's been a lot of carnage and mass murder out there. Anger takes us down the road of emotional murder.

> WE HATE SOMEONE BECAUSE OF THEIR POLITICS OR THE WORDS THEY SAID, UNWILLING TO FORGIVE THEM; BUT WHAT ABOUT BEING ABLE TO FORGIVE IN LIGHT OF ACTUAL MURDER?

We hate someone because of their politics or the words they said, unwilling to forgive them; but what about being able to forgive in light of actual murder?

In October 2006, Charles Roberts burst into a one-room Amish schoolhouse and shot ten young girls, killing five of them before killing himself. Nothing about it made sense, and the rage that had been in the shooter's heart quickly transferred to the nation's heart as the story broke. Who would do such a thing and why?

The Amish community chose a different path, though, one that didn't continue with anger. They didn't point fingers or blame anyone. Instead, they reached out to the killer's family and offered grace and kindness, comforting the Roberts family. A large crowd of Amish even came to Roberts' funeral.

The authors of *Amish Grace: How Forgiveness Transcended Tragedy*[10] revealed not only the powerful story of forgiveness from that event, but how a refusal to hold onto grudges and anger is a crucial part of Amish culture.

It's not part of our culture, but can you imagine if it were?

WHAT IS ANGER?

There are a lot of reasons we get angry. And in some cases, it's okay to feel that way. There's injustice, abuse, cheating, and all kinds of reasons we become angry. But whatever else anger is, it has a big mouth that will swallow us whole if we hold onto it too long. In that story of the two brothers, God warned Cain to be careful. "Sin is crouching at your door; it desires to have you, but you must rule over it" (Gen 4:7 NIV).

There is a time for anger, when anger is appropriate. But there is also anger that is incredibly destructive.

---

[10] *Amish Grace: How Forgiveness Transcended Tragedy* by Donald Kraybill, Steven Nolt, and David L. Weaver-Zercher.

When Anger Is Good

It would be easier if we could simply say anger is bad. But that's not the case.

More than once a woman has come to me for counseling due to a domestic abuse situation; and as she describes what's going on, I can feel the anger pouring out of her.

Somewhere in the midst of it, she stops. "I'm sorry," she says apologetically. "I know I shouldn't feel this way."

"Absolutely you should," I tell her. "If you weren't angry, I'd be worried."

Anger is one of the most complex emotions because it's not necessarily a wrong one. Even God gets angry. Anger isn't strictly a human emotion.

In Exodus 43:6–7, God tells Moses that He is compassionate and gracious, slow to anger; but He doesn't leave the guilty unpunished. This is God speaking about *Himself*. Over and over we're told that He is slow to anger, and we repeatedly see the forgiveness of God. Yet He does not let the guilty go unpunished. His anger will result in just punishment at some point because He is a righteous judge who is angry at sin every day (Psalm 7). We get angry when someone takes our parking spot. Imagine being God, seeing every wicked act ever committed (Proverbs 15:3).

God's anger is perfectly informed; we want Him to get angry.

In my reading, I came across a quote from a psychologist who said that anger often comes from the fear that we are being dealt with unjustly. Imagine how God feels when He sees the downright evil of human trafficking or the poor and vulnerable being ruthlessly exploited for purely selfish reasons. This aspect of God is difficult to understand if our image of Jesus Christ is some laid-back guy with long hair blowing in the wind, stepping off of a surfboard holding a lamb.

Proper anger leads to healing, resolution, and justice.

What if God's people got angry for the right reasons and with God's perspective, instead of the wrong reasons?

In Mark 3, we read of a man whose hand had been shriveled for a long time. Like many of the other people with physical disabilities and injuries, he was at the synagogue. That's where his path crossed with Jesus.

Powerful religious leaders were there, watching Jesus closely, because it was the Sabbath. They wanted to see if He'd heal anyone, which according to their law, was unlawful to do on the Sabbath.

"Stand up in front of everyone," Jesus told the man. Imagine being that man, hiding your disability for most of your life, now being asked to show it to everyone. But he obeyed.

Jesus, knowing what the religious leaders were thinking, threw a question out to everyone in earshot. "Which is lawful on the Sabbath, to do good or to do evil? To save life or to kill?"

Crickets. No one said a word. Jesus's words hung in the air as he looked around at them.

But here's the key: Jesus looked at them in *anger*. Their stubborn, calloused hearts were distressing to Him. "Stretch out your hand," He told the man, who obeyed, and he was completely healed.

It was now the religious leaders' turn to be angry, and they were. They left the scene and began plotting how to kill Jesus.

God's anger brings restoration and wholeness. Man's anger seeks to destroy someone who is perceived as an enemy (James 1:20). Just take a glance at our information sources, and it's easy to see anger being used as a tool to manipulate the masses or their particular audience. This philosophy is even condensed for a bumper sticker that says, "If you're not angry, you're not paying attention." If we are not discerning, those kinds of ideas can lead to dangerous ends.

The righteous anger that God has is good, and some of us need to get angry about what's happened to us, about the injustice we experienced. We shouldn't be so quick to make peace with injustice. Instead, we need to be willing to be deeply stirred about the things that stir God's heart.

Anger is not necessarily a sin, though it can lead us to doing something sinful (Ephesians 4:26). Only when we have the heart of God are we able to handle anger rightly.

When Anger Is Not Good

Not long ago, I spent my day off with a man who was headed to jail. He was a sharp guy, very smart and self-disciplined. But his wife knew exactly where his buttons were. She knew exactly how to push them, and when. And so she did. She was angry, and she wanted him to engage.

"You should be home more! You should work less! This isn't fair!" she said, pushing, pushing, pushing.

What she didn't realize was that, for this man, his response to anger was fight or flight. And if some guy was talking to this man like that, four inches from his face, he would either throw a punch or walk away to avoid doing something he would regret later.

The man turned around and walked away from the woman. He saw that as a noble action. But she saw it as not caring.

"Oh, now you don't care!" she screamed, throwing more words at greater volume, following him.

He turned around and grabbed her arm roughly. It scared her deeply and left two wounded people trying to figure out what was happening to their marriage. When our anger doesn't mirror God's anger, things get ugly.

Anger leads to sin when it is motivated by pride, when it's never dealt with and allowed to linger and fester unrestrained, or when it's no longer attacking the problem but is instead attacking the person.

Human anger has the unique attribute of being able to shut down anything meaningful that would help dissipate that anger. We're incapable of having honest and important conversations when we're emotionally raging inside because it colors everything we think and say. Human anger ends communication, and nothing productive comes from it.

Not everyone has seen the same kinds of anger. Growing up it might have been yelling or punching holes in the doors. Or it might have been a deliberate silence, a type of anger that refuses to communicate or engage in a productive way. It might have been anger that kept people around you walking on eggshells.

I'd be willing to say we've all been on the giving and receiving end of anger however it appears. And in most cases, it was unhealthy. It shut down areas of our life, and it shut us down emotionally.

We stopped trusting the angry person.

We stopped telling the truth to the angry person.

I see this all the time in marriage. When one person responds in anger, there are only two outcomes: the anger escalates and there's a fight, or the other person checks out. They might walk away to avoid a fight; but to an angry person, that action seems like indifference or apathy. Anger is like kryptonite to any relationship. No one is drawn to anger. No one softens or changes their mind in the face of anger. Anger hardens us because we're afraid we're going to lash out or be hurt by someone else. Anger blocks meaningful relationships.

Conflict, however, is part of life on planet Earth; and it does not have to be destructive. Les Parrot says, "Conflict is the price we pay for a deeper level of intimacy."[11] It has been described as the moment "when two opposing ideas or expectations collide." Those ideas are often embodied in living people! The Psychologist Carl Jung saw conflict from two perspectives. He said, "Conflicts create the fire of affects and emotions; and like every fire it has two aspects: that of burning and that of giving light."[12] In other words, conflict can be a friend when it helps us to see what is important more clearly.

---

[11] "Marriage Counselor Dr. Les Parrott Offers Tips for a Stronger Relationship," Newport Beach Independent, accessed April 10, 2024, https://www.newportbeachindy.com/marriage-counselor-dr-les-parrott-offers-tips-for-a-stronger-relationship/.

[12] 1. Carl Jung, "The Collected Works of C. G. Jung" (Princeton: Princeton University Press, 1960), 123.

We can come out the other side with a deeper understanding of each other. It is not my friend, though, if it burns us horribly in the process.

I often describe four typical styles of how angry people operate during conflict in a relationship. They might be a cowboy type, loud and boisterous, fighting and yelling and making a lot of noise. They are good at getting their emotions out, but there is often a lot of mess to clean up afterwards. Or, they are an ice king or queen, folding inward and going cold, punishing the other person with silence. Or they act as a doormat, allowing the presence of anger to shut down any honest expression of hopes and desires, acquiescing to the other person in every way, just to keep the peace. This can seem helpful in the short term, but what we attempt to bury has a high rate of resurrection. What has been smoldering beneath the surface eventually comes out in very extreme or distorted ways. Or worst of all is the terrorist type of person who is bent on just blowing the whole thing up so nobody wins.

None of those approaches is a laughing matter. I believe that it's almost impossible to act redemptively towards someone I'm angry with. When I read the Sermon on the Mount, it's clear that responding in the opposite spirit is a mark of God's grace being present and operating in our lives. Love your enemies, go the extra mile, forgive as you want to be forgiven and take the log out of your own eye first—these aren't some kind of warm, sappy philosophical notions but are rather very practical steps to being an agent of healing in a broken world. We need a better way to handle anger, both internally and when we're faced with someone who is angry.

LIVING A LIFE WITHOUT ANGER

We were seated around a table early one morning with a group of leaders discussing how to deal with a difficult issue we were all responsible for resolving. It was becoming obvious to everyone that the director of the team was bothered by how the conversation was going. As his emotional temperature gauge grew hotter, the discomfort level grew amongst the team; and everyone started to go quiet. It was then that he jumped to his feet and verbally unloaded on one of the men next to him. Keep in mind we were supposed to be friends and teammates. There was an awkward silence for a moment; and then my friend on his left gently touched his arm, looked him square in the eye and said, "Tom, I want to know where all this anger is coming from." The leader looked dumbfounded and without a word stormed out of the meeting.

Anger might seem like just a little monster in the room that we can manage, but it'll keep kicking us until we deal with it. It really is like the red light on the dashboard telling us to check the engine. It's not a bad thing, necessarily; but it's an indicator that something else is going on in our lives, something happening deep inside of us.

> THE FIRST STEP TO LIVING A LIFE THAT ISN'T STEEPED IN ANGER IS TO SIMPLY BE AWARE OF OUR ANGER PROBLEM. FROM THERE WE'RE POSITIONED TO TAKE THE NEXT STEPS.

Most people aren't in touch with this in their own lives. The first step to living a life that isn't steeped in anger is to simply be aware of our anger problem. From there we're positioned to take the next steps.

Avoid Angry People

We don't always know what makes a person angry. Some people blame it on genetics, for example, saying they get angry because they're a certain ethnicity or because they were just born with a short fuse or they picked it up from someone else's personality—we have all kinds of justifications for our anger.

Some people will make it impossible to handle anger properly because they are marinated in anger. Everything they say or do comes from a place of smoldering emotions. They are so consumed with it that it's almost impossible to know anything else about them—their personality, their interests, their thoughts—other than they are angry. We live in a polarized culture right now where everyone is angry at someone or about something. Throw a dart at Facebook, and you'll find one of those people.

We already know that we are blessed by who we *avoid* spending significant time with, refusing to walk with the wicked and hang out with mockers (Psalm 1:1). The same applies to perpetually angry people. God tells us to not make friends with a hot-tempered person and to not even associate with someone who is easily angered (Proverbs 22:24–25). We won't change them; they will more than likely change us.

Kill Anger Before It Kills You

Anger is emotional adrenaline.

Adrenaline is there for a reason. It helps us perform in a scary or difficult situation. But our bodies weren't meant to function with adrenaline constantly present, and neither are our emotions meant to function with anger constantly present. When anger is in the room, it poisons the environment. Everyone becomes tense.

Anger also creates real adrenaline in our physical body.

Anger hits parts of our brain before we're even aware of it, triggering a stress response and flooding your body with cortisol and adrenaline.[13] That means a life of anger is also one of increased heart attack and stroke risk, along with reduced immune response and increased anxiety.[14]

Our bodies aren't designed to function constantly with adrenaline; and over time, adrenaline can actually destroy the muscle tissue that is our heart. It destroys blood vessels and raises our blood pressure.

And it gets worse.

Repeated or regular anger results in a brain that has increased cognitive deficits, which over time will start to change

---

[13] "Brain: How Anger Affects Your Brain and Body [Infographic – Part 1]." NICABM. Accessed January 15, 2024. Available from: https://www.nicabm.com/brain-how-anger-affects-your-brain-and-body-part-1/.

[14] "7 Ways Anger Is Ruining Your Health." Everyday Health, 23 Jul 2014, https://www.everydayhealth.com/news/ways-anger-ruining-your-health/.

how we think.[15] Those altered patterns of thinking actually make continued anger more likely, causing us to do foolish things (Proverbs 14:17) we wouldn't do if we were thinking clearly. Being quick to anger causes us to make mistakes (Proverbs 14:29).

The self-perpetuating fog of anger is a difficult trap to get out of, but that's exactly what God tells us to do. We're to get rid of all the bitterness, passion, and anger, and stop shouting and insulting people, filling our lives and those around us with hateful feelings (Ephesians 4:31).

So how do we kill anger?

Start by avoiding what causes it whenever possible. If anger is a problem for you, it's time to consider ways to cut out the sources of anger wherever possible. God literally tells us to avoid foolish and ignorant arguments that are going to end up in an angry fight (2 Timothy 2:23–25). Whether it's social media, watching cable news, listening to your go-to political commentators, or even interacting with the guy at the water cooler at work who likes to push your buttons—consider what makes you angry the most often and try fasting from it for a season to see what happens to the condition of your mind and soul. There may be something valuable to be gained from jumping off the crazy train of public opinion.

Then, make a habit of being quick to listen and speaking less, like we covered in the previous chapter. Listening first

---

[15] Zachar, R. M. (n.d.). The Angry Brain. Retrieved January 15, 2024, from https://div12.org/the-angry-brain/.

and speaking less help us become slow to anger (James 1:19–20). And by listening, I mean not simply waiting for a person to pause for a breath before you launch into a tirade on all the ways they're wrong. I mean actually *listening* and considering what they are saying. Try feeding back to them what you think you just heard them say. Ask more questions than you might think are necessary. This is especially helpful when there is a real or perceived injustice driving the emotions. The goal isn't to settle a score but to know and be known to each other. When you do speak, choose your words carefully, wanting to build them up instead of tear them down (Ephesians 4:29).

Instead of letting anger get the best of you, conquer it by doing good instead (Romans 12:21). Be willing to ignore those who have offended your sensibilities (Proverbs 19:11). Choose not to get revenge, even just wanting to have the last word (Romans 12:19). Pray for others, particularly those who make you angry; you might be surprised to discover that it's very difficult to remain angry with someone you're sincerely praying for (1 Timothy 2:8).

In Ephesians 4:26–27, Paul equates prolonged anger to giving the enemy a foothold in our lives. Holding onto anger is like allowing a squatter to reside in your basement. They have no right to be there, but they will stay until they're evicted.

Go a Different Way

In marriage counseling, I often end up with two angry people going back and forth across the table. They're so angry, but they can't explain why. Their relationship has completely broken down, and they're currently just running on symptoms of all that baggage.

How did that couple who ended up in a physical fight get to the point where the husband was arrested? That's a question they should be asking themselves. If they carefully deconstructed it, could they figure out how to not get there again?

When I'm working with someone struggling with a sexual temptation, it starts with a simple conversation: when are you most likely to watch porn?

"When I'm alone on my computer in a room by myself and my wife's gone to bed," the guy might say.

"Okay, here are some practical tips," I reply. "Go to bed when your wife goes to bed."

"I can't fall asleep."

"Use your computer in a public space, like the kitchen."

"I can't do that because I don't get anything done."

At some point it's clear they don't want to find answers or solutions. They want a different result, but they want to stick with their current path.

Years ago, a high school student shared with his youth pastor that he was struggling with lust. Each week he'd come to my friend with a new concern involving him and his girlfriend and how quickly things were progressing, and each week he would tell him to do something practical. Stay away from all forms of porn. Do not use the internet alone. Carefully monitor what you watch. Refuse be alone with your girlfriend in a private place. Commit to practical action steps.

Each week he'd be upset because the lust problem didn't go away. Finally, he came to my friend in a panic because he'd had sex with his girlfriend, and now she was pregnant. The youth pastor reached into his pockets and pulled out a container of Tic Tacs.

"Hold out your hand," he said, dropping four white Tic Tacs into the student's hand. "There you go."

"What's this for?"

"Dude, I gave you the *best* advice I could think of, and you didn't take any of it. So, that's all I have left to give you, a few mints," the youth pastor said. "I hope that helps." My friend wasn't trying to be cruel, but he was trying to help this young man see what he was blind to. "If you are wise, your wisdom will reward you; if you are a mocker, you alone will suffer" (Proverbs 9:12).

He refused wise and practical counsel, and now he was simply going to eat the fruit of his ways until he yielded his heart to God's design. I am absolutely certain that Jesus can forgive the darkest sin and cleanse us from all unrighteousness. No sin has the power to trump His grace. Yet there are times when He allows the consequences to run their course in our lives, and He will use those to accomplish something deeper. In *The Great Divorce*, C. S. Lewis wrote that hell is the place we go because God gives us what we want. Our will be done. If we never stop to deconstruct what keeps bringing us to anger and choose a different path, we will keep doing it. A rut, someone once said, is the path of least resistance. If we are honest, we will see that a lot of what we struggle with is actually a well-worn path of behaviors in how we react to others. People don't just wake up one morning planning a road rage incident. But in the moment of perceived offense, they have a hair-trigger reaction to what they see as a personal injustice. The way to move forward is to confront those emotional ruts together with a grace-giving, truth-telling, transformational God.

> THE WAY TO MOVE FORWARD IS TO CONFRONT THOSE EMOTIONAL RUTS TOGETHER WITH A GRACE-GIVING, TRUTH-TELLING, TRANSFORMATIONAL GOD.

We can't put on a new life unless we put away the old one (Ephesians 4:22–24). We can't keep doing the same things over and expect to arrive at the end with a new result. Getting stuck in the middle between the old life and new life is the most miserable of all, unable to enjoy heaven and unable to enjoy hell.

Why are you angry? How did you get there? Are you always fired up, ready to be angry in a flash, body flooded with adrenaline?

SHOWING COMPASSION INSTEAD OF ANGER

If anger is the poison that consumes everyone in the room and is the kryptonite of relationships, what is its antidote?

The right kind of anger has, as noted, two elements: First, it has to be based on God and tempered in mercy. It can't be my agenda. It has to be God's. This is important because the second aspect is that it must be mixed with a heart of grief.

On the opposite side of anger is compassion.

Compassion lets us see others as God sees them, treating them how God would treat them. It means feeling deeply what someone else is feeling. Remember, God told us He was slow to anger and quick to compassion. We operate in reverse, quick to anger and slow (if ever) to compassion.

Compassion is uncomfortable because it stretches our heart, which will never go back to its original shape. It gives us access to the heart of God. Empathy is an awareness of other people's emotional experiences and an attempt to feel those same emotions from their perspective. Compassion, however, is fueled by the desire to take action to actually help the other person. The word compassion literally means "to suffer together." Compassion happens when we step into the lives of people and see them as human beings instead of a faceless demographic or stereotype. The moment we take that step, anger becomes very difficult to hold onto. I am now living proactively instead of reactively.

Think about this in light of all the strife we currently see between the ethnic groups in our country. Or how about the immigration debate? Or between the haves and the have nots? Or between the sexes? Or just about any social issue that is producing turmoil around us. What if we could be empowered to slow down and feel what they feel from their perspective? It would revolutionize our society! Most of the time, people are protesting because they don't feel heard or seen by the power brokers. They don't feel like they have a voice that matters.

This is what I love about the message of the Gospel. God slowed down and became one of us for thirty-three years. He suffered injustice, He was misunderstood, He was judged unrighteously, He was hated without a cause. God gets us. The cross says to every man and woman on the planet, "I understand how you feel." The cross says "No one has the right to hold a grudge against another. I went first in forgiveness so now come follow me."

Compassion doesn't excuse the sin. It doesn't say that something is right when it's wrong. What I'm talking about is the condition of our hearts. Can we be angry and not sin? That's only possible when we have God's heart.

In John 8, we read of a woman who had been caught cheating on her husband, and the law of the land in those days was to stone her to death. Dropping her to the ground like a pile of discarded bones, the religious leaders thought they could trap Jesus.

"She was caught in the act of adultery," they said triumphantly. "The law of Moses says to stone her. What do you say?"

"Let any of you who is without sin throw the first stone at her," He said.

The first of the crowd to walk away were the older men. The younger eventually followed, dropping their stones to the ground as Jesus told the woman to go and sin no more.

Why did the older men leave first?

Because the more life you live, the more you realize how many times you've needed compassion shown to you. We have been humbled by our failures, and we are aware that we are not as superior as we may have thought when zeal alone ruled our lives.

God's grief when Cain killed his brother Abel was real, but so was His compassion on Cain that even in His just punishment of banishing him, He promised to protect Cain.

God promises to settle all accounts; it's not up to us to get revenge (Romans 12:17–21). We live in the tension of being in an unjust world where what we experience can hurt. But that doesn't change who God is, and He will have the last word. Our anger has no place in that final say.

CHAPTER EIGHT REFLECTIONS:
NAVIGATING CONFLICT AND ANGER

1) What kind of circumstances "push your buttons?" Where do you find that your anger gauge starts to rise and why? Is there a place farther back that those emotions are coming from?

2) How would you describe your style of conflict when you find that you're disagreeing with someone? Are you aware of how you are being perceived? Your words? Your body language?

3) What kind of questions can you ask each other when you find yourself in the middle of a conflict? Where might there be a new understanding that would help you both get unstuck? What would you like the person to ask you that would be helpful and make you feel like you are being seen and heard?

CHAPTER NINE

A Heart Condition

"When you're born, you're like a key with no cuts in it. As you go through life, each wound, failure, hurt … cuts into that strip of metal. And one day there is a clear click—your pain has formed the key that slips into the lock that opens your future."
–T. D. Jakes

"We are all mere beggars telling other beggars where to find bread."
– Martin Luther

"Above all else, guard your heart, for everything you do flows from it."
– Proverbs 4:23 (NIV)

We were playing basketball, but really it was more like guerilla ball. A bunch of guys, some playing a much younger game than their knees could take, acting as if the national championship was on the line.

Things were getting rough out on the court; and at a critical moment in the game, I learned an important lesson.

Bam!

Either I hit a wall or a wall hit me. I dropped to the floor, confused for a moment, wondering what had happened.

"Hey man, are you okay?" I heard. I looked down and saw that my arm was all cut up. These guys meant business out on the court.

Sitting on the bench to take a breather and regather my senses, hoping some of the stinging in my arm would go away so I could catch a few more hoops before the night was over, I watched the other guys playing and a strange thought popped into my head. *"I'm just gonna sit here until the guy who knocked me out comes over and patches me up."*

Sounds crazy when you say that out loud, doesn't it? Because that's not how things work. But that's how we sometimes deal with our emotional injuries.

Someone does us wrong, it hurts, and we sit on the sidelines, nursing the pain. We wait for someone else—maybe the one who hurt us—to come along and make everything right.

But what if that person never shows up? What if they don't even realize they did any damage? Do we stay on the bench for the rest of our life, nursing the bleeding wound?

By then I wasn't really thinking about the cut on my arm or the shouts from the court or the basketball whizzing by my head now and then. A light bulb had gone off, and I saw forgiveness and healing in a different light.

We can't wait for someone else to fix what's broken. We can't wait for someone else to bandage our wounds.

In the *Andy Griffith Show*, Sheriff Andy Taylor and his deputy, Barney Fife, had a frequent flier in their town jail. Otis, who loved the bottle and was the town drunk, would wander into the police station a few times a week, grab the key from the wall, and lock himself in jail for public intoxication.

By morning, with a clearer head and a good night's rest, Otis would reach through the bars of the cell, grab the same key, and unlock himself. Waving a cheery goodbye, he'd walk out of the jail, free.

"See you next time, Otis!" Andy or Barney would tell him. "Say hi to your wife!"

No one put Otis in jail. He chose it himself. And while I wouldn't compare people to the town drunk who wobbled into jail on his own, the point is that he was a prisoner only as long as he chose to be. The key was always there, waiting for him to grab it and go.

Now go back to that basketball court, where I was hunched on the sidelines thinking deep thoughts and cradling my bloody arm, wincing. If I hadn't decided to get up and grab the key to healing (in this case, a bandage and some antiseptic cream), that wound would do what wounds do best: get infected.

Unchecked infections get into our blood, spreading throughout our entire body. In a few hours, we can die.

"Here lies Bruce, the victim of a basketball injury, unwilling to clean his own cut," the headstone would read.

Obviously, that would be silly. We all know to be smarter than that. Yet we do something just as illogical when it comes to our emotional wounds, those scars that are permanently settled around our hearts.

Those little hidden cuts are like a warp in an airplane wing. It has more impact than we ever imagined when it comes to pushing us off course or fighting against us as we try to stay true. Unresolved issues like guilt, shame, anger, and unforgiveness lead to destructive patterns that hurt us and the people we love.

Worse, unresolved issues create a cycle of infection and pain that becomes septic. Our entire lives are consumed in regret.

There's an antidote. There's a key hanging on the wall. Everything about it goes against our culture and human nature. But this antidote is tried and true.

And when we take it in, we have the keys to healing, personal growth, and a life without regret. There will still be pain; it's a broken world after all. But our scars can be redeemed.

SCARS TO STORIES

A woman in our church was losing her adult son to cancer. He was young and had a family and a great future. Before he passed away, he said to her, "Mom, live your minutes with meaning and purpose; it will only be a short time before we see each other again." His death was devastating for her. I saw how deep the pain went. But instead of living in the pain, she put it to work and became a grief counselor for others going through trauma and tragedy. And at age sixty, she has a tattoo on her forearm that says it all: "Live your minutes." Whenever she is asked about it, she shares that her wounds produced scars that in turn became a greater story.

She will tell you today that through the crushing grief, something beautiful came forth. Was it pleasant at the time? Of course not, but it brought life out of death. Scars tell our story; and over time if we let them, they actually become our strong point instead of our weak point. They aren't just a reminder of past hurts but a beacon that calls out to healing. They let others know what we've been through and that we've been *through* it. When our wounds no longer have power over us and become scars, we are given the power to help and comfort others (2 Corinthians 1:3–4). Just look around at any successful recovery program, and you will find that it is very likely led by once-broken people who experienced healing and life change. In turn, they now live to give back and help others discover what set them free.

> SCARS TELL OUR STORY; AND OVER TIME IF WE LET THEM, THEY ACTUALLY BECOME OUR STRONG POINT INSTEAD OF OUR WEAK POINT.

It's amazing when you think about it. God somehow keeps track of billions of individual stories and intertwines them at just the right moments. The potential and power of what happens when our wounds turn into scars, and then into our stories, is almost impossible to comprehend.

Yet the wounds we haven't dealt with continue to cripple us. A wound is a painful injury, susceptible to infection, that hurts when it's touched. If our inner wounds are not treated, they can lead to more chronic conditions such as bitterness and despair.

In *How Does God Change Us?* Dane Ortlund says, "There is nothing noble about staying in that pit of despair. Healthy despair is an intersection, not a highway; a gateway, not a pathway. We must go there. But we dare not stay there." Experiencing despair and pain is something we sometimes need to do because it is in those rock bottom, desert places that we are often humbled and come to the end of ourselves. In God's eyes, that is a good place to be. He delights to give grace to the humble and broken, but He withholds it from the arrogant and self-sufficient. So, we can't park ourselves in a place of pain forever. We can't let our wounds fester and live our lives in a place of brokenness. We have to see that with God what looks like a dead end may in fact be the beginning of a journey that we would have never imagined on our own.

Healing From Wounds

The story of Absalom is a tragic one that fills the pages of 2 Samuel. A favorite of his father, King David, and well-liked by the people of Israel, he was charming, good-looking, and in every way captivating. Everything about him seemed to exude strength and wholeness.

But after his sister, Tamar, was raped, Absalom's pain and rage knew no bounds. He arranged to have her rapist murdered, which led to isolation from his family for a time. Eventually, he tried to lead a revolt to become king, and was murdered while he hung helplessly from a tree.

Absalom was living his life through a wound. He was not whole. He was not healed. He was not using his hurt to help others. Instead, his wound led to revenge, plotting, scheming, and ultimately death. He let those who had wounded him determine his future.

We are often faced with people who are speaking and living life through their pain. The condition of their heart is shaped by what wounded them, and that often defines how they see or live life.

Healing can be a cheap word in the church. We throw it around a lot, both as a descriptive and prescriptive word. But what does it mean to heal from a wound, especially those that aren't visible? How do we recognize the effect of a wound that's been ignored in someone's life, a wound that's festering and spilling infection into other parts of their life? How do we know when it's healed? Is the pain gone?

It would be great if the person who hurt you would come to you, apologize profusely, and do everything to make it right; but as I pointed out earlier, that rarely happens.

What if the person who hurt you is gone? What if there's no chance for confrontation or closure? Do you stay in prison for the rest of your life?

These are hard questions, but I have to ask them because this is the reality for many. Oftentimes as a pastor, I'll realize someone has a wound that hasn't healed.

I'll ask them, "As a pastor, as a husband, as a father and as a man—I want to ask for your forgiveness on behalf of whoever did this to you." It's not uncommon that they break down and weep because they've been waiting a long time to hear that from their husband, father, or whoever might have hurt them. But they might never hear it because the one who wounds us rarely comes back to fix things.

The key to healing isn't always about getting an apology or even confronting those things of the past. Instead, it's finding a way to let go. This is not some hollow or fatalistic exercise. It is a courageous and faith-filled act of forgiveness. It has often been described as surrendering into God's hands the legitimate right that I have to justice. He is the One who will finish the story on my behalf.

Can we release the hold that the wounds have on us? Can we choose to heal, to step off the sidelines of the basketball court, and to go find the bandages and things that will bring healing?

For our wounds to heal and our scars to become stories, the goal isn't to forget or ignore the pain. Instead, it's about taking control of the narrative.

You say to yourself, "Yes, this happened to me. But that's not all I am. That's not my identity."

When we acknowledge what happened, face it, and then show our scars and share the stories, what we actually do is let others know they aren't alone and that there is hope.

Even when the circumstances aren't ideal, healing is possible. Not necessarily quick, but possible. It's about taking steps toward a place in life where the pain doesn't control us. We know that we are becoming whole again when our past no longer dictates our present state of mind. Rather it becomes a reference point to look back upon as we continue our journeys forward.

We might remember the pain. It might surprise us once in a while with a visit. But it no longer determines who we will be.

Changing Your Perspective on Pain

Nick Vujicic was born without arms and legs.

His literal perspective is very different from most people's, but so is how he might view daily life. His disability could define him, and who would argue that he has limits? He couldn't be expected to accomplish everything someone with arms and legs could do, right?

It's not as if Vujicic didn't struggle with negative emotions, but he chose to take a different perspective on life. He put on a different mindset and has made a name traveling the world as a motivational speaker, encouraging people in their faith and giving them a reason to hope.

Our perspective doesn't change without a fight. There's a default state that the world reverts to, that we revert to, when we're experiencing pain. It's often one of victimhood, revenge, and grudges that keeps the wounds fresh. This is the fatal flaw that keeps the peoples of the world at war with one another throughout generations.

Perspective matters. Are you stuck on bedrest or is it a chance to finally catch up on your reading? Are you feeling physical pain, or is it a chance to pray for others experiencing the same thing? Are you broke, or is it a chance to show your love by giving the gift of your time and presence instead of buying a gift at the store?

Seeing things from a different point of view makes all the difference. We should be in a constant state of refreshing the perspective we have instead of conforming to how the world (even well-meaning people) tells us we should see our situation (Ephesians 4:23, Romans 12:2).

Instead of talking about pain in terms of hurt, I want to try a different angle. What if we saw pain as not just something miserable to endure and get through, but as a catalyst for growth?

A catalyst is anything that speeds up a chemical reaction or lowers the temperature or pressure that's necessary to start that reaction, without being consumed during the process of the reaction. In a story, a catalyst is any moment or inciting incident that gets some kind of conflict or action set in motion. Without it, the story wouldn't exist; there'd be no story to tell.

When we see pain as a catalyst instead of something awful to endure or avoid, it takes on new life.

T.D. Jakes describes that process as our lives being like a key. Life is full of different cuts. Those cuts are ground into the key, and there doesn't seem to be a pattern or reason. Maybe it seems a bit too much. But God knows that one day, there's going to be a locked door before us, and our lives will be the exact fit to open that door.

No key, no open door.

If we only see pain as unnecessary hurt, we rush through the healing or find ways to dull or avoid the pain. It becomes a festering wound instead of the catalyst God intended.

When we see pain as God sees it, it changes from being a journey of survival to a journey to freedom, to a new place we would have never imagined going before.

Confronting and Overcoming Regret

Regret is always connected to the past, never the future. It's looking back and feeling sorrow and disappointment about things we wish were different but cannot possibly change. It's that foolish choice we made that destroyed our family or the bad decision that blew up the business—whatever it is, we look back and feel pain. Whether the wound is our own or someone else's doing, it sits in the past and constantly calls out to us to go back to it and hurt all over again.

> THE ONLY THING WE CAN DO WITH REGRET RIGHT NOW, IN THE PRESENT, IS CHOOSE TO LET IT BE AN ANCHOR OR AN ENGINE.

The only thing we can do with regret right now, in the present, is choose to let it be an anchor or an engine.

I often talk about the wisdom of decision-making. "What's the wise thing to do here?" is a question I encourage people to get in the habit of asking themselves. It doesn't matter if it's relationships, finances, or "what's next for me in life?" Starting from this question helps reduce future regrets because it forces us to consider the consequences of our actions and align decisions with our faith and values.

But what about the regrets we already carry? We can't go back and have a do-over.

I read a story of a man (like many of us) who was well-informed on what things were unhealthy. Yet despite knowing the potential risks to his health, he made decisions and formed habits that were harming him. He knew it but didn't choose to stop.

Then the day came when he had a serious heart attack. Now he was scared. Now he was taking all of that information and putting it to work in his life, making the right decisions. For him, change didn't happen without a scare, until he was forced to experience and confront the consequences of his behavior. He lived his life differently going forward. He didn't want to view his past with regret; instead, he saw the scare as the thing that got him to change.

That's the turning point, that shift in our perspective. That's where we confront and overcome our regrets. That's where we stop punishing ourselves for our mistakes. That's where we accept the forgiveness offered on the cross. We make that forgiveness our own, and then we act as if we're really living in that forgiveness going forward. Forgiveness, someone has said, is giving up any hope for a better past.

When we get this wrong, our regrets don't drive us forward but sideways. We are so filled with regret, shame, and guilt that we look for false comfort someplace else. Food, alcohol, bad relationships, shopping—these dull the pain we feel when confronted with regret, but only for a moment. They quickly add to the burden and make the pain worse.

In the Old Testament one of the idols that the Philistines worshiped was called Beelzebub. His name means "the lord of the flies." What an interesting name for a demon. Flies feed off of corrupted material, dead stuff. Whenever Israel was tempted into worshiping this idol it was because something had died in their relationship with the living God. That idol worship always produced more corruption and death. That same enemy of God swarms to our wounds to see where he can take further advantage of our fallenness. Don't give up more time or ground to him.

When you look back, what are your regrets? What do you wish you'd done differently? It's good to confront regrets; but when you do, you have to decide if you'll make a change going forward or just delay the change and go sideways.

We have to make peace with our past without letting it control our present and future. Using what we learned from our regrets helps us become better versions of ourselves.

THE DANGER OF HARDENED HEARTS

In the herbal remedy world, comfrey and plantain are known for their incredible healing properties. But which one to use depends on the kind of wound.

Comfrey, sometimes called knitbone, is an aggressive healer. Helping with infection and cell growth, it can help heal a wound very quickly. Plantain (the weed, not the fruit) is also great for healing wounds, but it works at a slower pace and is better suited for deeper wounds.

Now, that might seem strange. Wouldn't you want faster healing, especially for a deep wound? No. Because comfrey can heal so quickly, it can lock in an infection, closing up the surface and making everything look great while there's poison lurking below.

Remember the young woman who had been abused by her uncle as a child? She seemed to heal up quickly and beautifully, living an amazing and productive life. That is, until something poked that wound, one she didn't even realize she still had. She thought she had healed up. She'd developed coping mechanisms that had worked for years.

Except what had happened is that she had allowed her heart to be hardened. When something wounds us deeply enough, we want the surface to heal up quickly. A hard heart seems like a great defense, making it possible for surface healing to happen. Nothing gets past that scar tissue, even though there's still an infection lurking below.

For this reason, a wounded heart easily becomes a hard heart, especially if it is wounded over and over, scar tissue building on top of scar tissue. And a hard heart can't experience the amazing things God has for us. It can't accept the gifts and blessings He wants in our lives. The gifts go right by us, and we miss out because we're wounded and trying to live as if we weren't.

Imagine it's Christmas morning and the entire family is gathered in the living room. The lights are on the tree, the kitchen smells like turkey dinner, and maybe there's a hint of ginger cookies. Soft music is playing. It seems as if, for one moment, everyone is happy.

Everyone, except little Becky.

She sits quietly on the floor just a bit further from the tree than the other children. As the gifts are handed out, she shakes her head no. She doesn't want the gifts that have her name on them.

"Becky, what's wrong?" her mother asks, concerned. She places her wrist on the girl's forehead to see if she has a fever, wondering if she might be sick.

"I'm fine," Becky replies. "I just don't want the gifts."

The entire family stops tearing open their packages and stares at her. Who wouldn't want a gift?

"Last year I didn't get what I wanted and was so disappointed that I'd rather not open any gifts this year," she says. "This way I won't be disappointed again."

That is ridiculous, of course. We all enjoy getting gifts. But when we harden our heart because of a hurt that someone has caused us, we end up missing out on the gifts God has for us. We're just like Becky.

As a pastor, I've come across many forms of this kind of heart condition. How it appears varies. It might manifest as guilt, shame, anger, envy, unforgiveness, perceived injustice, or disappointment. These aren't just fleeting emotions, but symptoms of something deep, something that needs healing.

Guilt and shame keep us from enjoying God's forgiveness. Anger and envy rob us of peace and joy. And unforgiveness ties us permanently to the past, never letting us move forward. These might be emotional wounds, but they affect our health

(Proverbs 14:30). Emotional and spiritual turmoil eat away at our bodies.

If pain is a catalyst, if pain can change our life, if pain is God disciplining us because He loves us (Hebrews 12:6), if a wound can create a scar that can create a story that will help others ... hardening our hearts wastes all of it.

Everything we do flows out of our hearts (Proverbs 4:23). It's not a question of whether you're being a good person today. The heart condition is what drives everything we think, speak, and do. Don't underestimate the results of a fearful or angry heart.

The Trap of Entitlement

It's not just wounds that create hardened hearts. A sense of entitlement will do the trick, too. What starts with humility and gratitude can quickly lead to entitlement if we're not careful.

I once heard a pastor speaking at a convention of thousands of leaders say, "the sure downfall of people in ministry is when they feel like they have the right to touch the gold, the girls, and God's glory." That is the sound of entitlement. We think we live above the principles that ought to define our lives.

I had a friend who was hired by a large church as a consultant. They were having some issues and thought an outside perspective could help sort things out. They flew him in, and he listened to the leaders discuss various topics at a board meeting. After an hour or so, the board turned to the consultant.

"Do you have anything you'd like to say?" they asked him.

"I just have one question," he said. Turning to the pastor, he asked, "Who around this table has the power and the right to say no to you and you can't go against it?"

The pastor thought for a moment and then said, "No one. I'm the CEO."

The consultant started to gather his things to leave.

"Where are you going?" they asked him.

"I'm leaving," he said. "I can't do anything here."

Someone with a hard heart is someone who is no longer willing to listen. It's someone who thinks in terms of knowing the right to do something instead of whether it is beneficial to do something.

And like those who have hard hearts from wounds, the entitled person will miss out on the gifts God intended. Not only that, but a proud heart will inevitably be brought low (Proverbs 16:18). Just look around at leadership in any arena of life, be it church, politics, or business; and you see this principle is true. It's just a matter of time. Yet, God's mercy is so deep and His love so great that He provides multiple opportunities to soften us and rescue us from that hardened state. No one wins with a hard heart.

Disappointment and Hope

In the light of some kinds of wounds, little disappointments here and there might seem unimportant. When people are giving their testimonies of big tragedies that have happened in their lives, it can seem embarrassing to be so wounded by what seems like a paper cut.

Then there's the idea of death by a thousand paper cuts, that horrifying slow death that's more painful because your blood drips out little by little over time.

Disappointment is like that.

It comes in big moments, that's true; but it also creeps up on soft feet throughout the day, so small and quiet we don't always register the wound. Little by little, things we hoped for are chipped away.

Hope deferred makes the heart sick (Proverbs 13:12). Experiencing disappointment of any kind can, over time, create incredible wounds. Our ability to acknowledge disappointment and deal with it the right way matters; disappointment can either fester into bitterness or soften the heart.

In a private letter, C. S. Lewis warned against seeking consolation in resentment when faced with disappointment. "It is a favorite desire of the human mind," he wrote, and it's "… the only way in which an early failure like this can become a real permanent injury."[16]

Hope deferred hurts. But strangely, it can either tenderize or harden the heart. Charles Spurgeon wrote, "The same sun which melts wax hardens clay. And the same Gospel which melts some persons to repentance hardens others in their sins."[17]

---

[16] Todd Stryd, "'He Knows All about It': C. S. Lewis and Psalm 103," Christian Counseling and Educational Foundation, April 17, 2023, https://www.ccef.org/he-knows-all-about-it-c-s-lewis-and-psalm-103.

[17] Charles Spurgeon, quoted in "The Metropolitan Tabernacle Pulpit," 1865, 11.

We live in an unjust world where oftentimes good people suffer and the foolish seem to prosper; the Bible is filled with faithful people who, through the ages, have asked God for an explanation. In fact, well over a third of the book of Psalms are songs and prayers of lament, the language they used when the storms of life rolled in. God was not put off by their questions. And while it's easy to get caught up in disappointment and unfairness, He constantly assured them that He would have the last word in their lives.

The beauty of all of the pain and injustice we experience in this life is that we can rest knowing that those things don't define our eternal story. The fleeting comforts and pain of this life will end. Our Father has promised to carry us when we cannot carry ourselves, and His eternal kingdom will one day make all things new.

> OUR FATHER HAS PROMISED TO CARRY US WHEN WE CANNOT CARRY OURSELVES, AND HIS ETERNAL KINGDOM WILL ONE DAY MAKE ALL THINGS NEW.

CHAPTER NINE REFLECTIONS:
FINDING STRENGTH THROUGH ADVERSITY

1) How would you rate yourself dealing with life's disappointments? Do they tip you over emotionally? How do they affect your heart's condition?

2) Can you think of a time when pain actually made you stronger or better in the end? If someone was to ask you to explain how that took place, how would you describe it?

3) Think about the scars that you carry in your life. How could God turn those to stories that might give someone else hope and courage to overcome? How could that actually become a part of your own healing journey?

4) Try taking a slow journey through the book of Psalms. Are there any chapters that seem to resonate with you or put into words what you're feeling?

CHAPTER TEN

*Allegiance to
the Kingdom*

"The great human dogma, then, is that the wind moves the trees. The great human heresy is that the trees move the wind."

– G.K Chesterton, *The Wind and the Trees*

"Who has ascended to heaven and come down? Who has gathered the wind in his fists? Who has wrapped up the waters in a garment? Who has established all the ends of the earth? What is his name, and what is his son's name? Surely you know!"

– Proverbs 30:4 (ESV)

Solomon was unique. There was never a ruler like Solomon. He was the richest, he was the wisest, he had the most material goods, and he was the most powerful. His kingdom was vast and was at peace. All the nations would come to see him because his wisdom was known far and wide. They would sit and listen to Solomon hold court, taking note of his magnificent architecture, his thousands of chariots, his stables of horses, and his women. They saw what the endless amounts of gold he'd accumulated had produced.

Solomon wrote in Proverbs 8 that the fear of the Lord (which is the beginning of wisdom) is to hate evil, pride, arrogance, and any such thing that damages body and soul. Here Solomon is, writing about the Kingdom of God, sitting on the throne of his own incredible empire; and in the next phase of his life, he writes Ecclesiastes, where the repeated thought is that it's all meaningless. What happened?

1 Kings chapter 11 tells us that somewhere along the way, he lost his heart. His wealth and his foreign wives turned his heart away from the God who had put him on the throne. He lost himself in the midst of it all.

God is the source of all authority, even of ungodly authority. It's not that ungodliness emanates from God but that He ordains it to be.

Consider the kingdom of Babylon and their king Nebuchadnezzar. Babylon was so full of evil, so idolatrous and rebellious, that in Revelation it is used to symbolize the anti-Christ kingdom. Yet God said to His people that because they had disobeyed Him, He would give them into the hands of His servant, Nebuchadnezzar. This was a king whose heart was set against God but was still used by God for God's purposes. It's a good reminder that, when it feels like the world is against us or there seems to be no hope because our leaders are a disaster, God can still make the mess serve His greater purposes. The Old Testament describes a long list of rulers ordained by God but ignorant of or in rebellion to His ways. They thought they held the power until God called them to account. I think this is what Solomon realized when he wrote, "The king's heart is like a stream of water directed by the LORD, he guides it wherever he pleases" (Proverbs 21:1 NLT).

God gives those leaders their breath. He allows them to be in a position of authority. And when God takes that breath away, they drop like any other man. Solomon is proof of that.

He had it completely right, and then he had it completely wrong. And then he was gone, just one more player in God's unfolding drama. When he stepped off the stage, both his heart and his kingdom were divided.

> ❧
>
> **GOD GIVES THOSE LEADERS THEIR BREATH. HE ALLOWS THEM TO BE IN A POSITION OF AUTHORITY. AND WHEN GOD TAKES THAT BREATH AWAY, THEY DROP LIKE ANY OTHER MAN.**
>
> ❧

THE CHARACTERISTICS OF A KINGDOM

There are three distinct characteristics to every kingdom. First, there has to be a king.

This is the person at the top. And according to the Bible, the King of Kings, the King of the Kingdom of God, has a name. His name is Jesus. And in the last days He's going to appear once again on the Earth to rule and to reign.

If we look at the nation we live in, we wouldn't call our president a king. We have a leader who's elected by the citizens. That's called a democracy, a form of government by the people and for the people. But not every nation agrees this is the best form of rule. There are over forty sovereign nations today who have a sovereign monarch as the head of state. If you ever visit one of those, you find that the people view their authority figures quite differently than those of us in the West. A kingdom might look like a corporation with a CEO who presides over everyone in his downline. Whatever the "kingdom" looks like, there is always someone at the top.

Second, the kingdom is dynamic. It is alive, always looking to assert its influence, always seeking to expand its borders, or—in the case of the corporation—its bottom line.

Third, a kingdom must have people in it, subjects who do the bidding of the king. Proverbs 14:28 says: "In a multitude of people is the glory of a king, but without people a prince is ruined." If you think you're a "king" but don't have anyone following you, you're just kidding yourself. John Maxwell says: "He who thinks he leads, but has no followers, is only taking a walk."

Not every kingdom is a place we'd want to be in because not every kingdom is led by a just and good king. And in a cyclical way, we follow as we are led.

A Good King with True Authority

Proverbs reveals that the characteristics of God are also the characteristics of a good government.

Good kings detest wrongdoing, and a throne should be established through righteousness (Proverbs 16:12). If the wicked influences are removed from the king's presence, his throne will be established through righteousness (Proverbs 25:5). By justice, a king gives stability to a nation, but those who are greedy for bribes will tear it down (Proverbs 29:4). A nation that is rebellious has many rulers, but a ruler with discernment and knowledge maintains order (Proverbs 28:2). And when the righteous are able to thrive, the people of a nation will rejoice. But when the wicked rule, the people will groan (Proverbs 29:2).

Righteousness. Discernment. Justice. Stability. Integrity. These are the characteristics that flow from the mind and heart of God. If you take them out of a king, out of a governor, out of whatever authority figure you can think of, what you end up with is injustice, mourning, groaning, and oppression.

Jesus told His disciples that all authority in heaven and on earth has been given to Him (Matthew 28:18). He then told those fishermen, those tax collectors, those average people, that they were being sent out in that authority.

"Go and make disciples. Make followers in all the nations, baptizing them in the name of the Father and the Son and the Holy Spirit. Teach them to obey everything I commanded you," Jesus told them.

That was very presumptuous of Jesus. Here was a group of men who didn't have much education, public esteem, or political influence. And yet Jesus conferred His authority onto them. He put His kingdom endorsement on them, giving them all of the authority He had to expand its influence.

It wasn't the first time He acknowledged who had real authority and who it was given to. When Jesus stood in front of Pilate, the Roman governor, Pilate demanded that He acknowledge that Pilate had the authority to free or crucify Jesus (John 19:10). Jesus' response was direct: Pilate had no authority over Him unless that authority was given to him from somewhere else.

King Jesus didn't puff up with pride, didn't become indignant, didn't call down fire from heaven to show Pilate up. He simply acknowledged that Pilate had authority over Him, but only because it was given to him by a greater authority. It wasn't arrogance or bravado, simply recognition.

Before Pilate, Jesus was completely secure in the truth. Do we find security knowing our true source of authority, or can one election send our world spinning?

Government Is for Your Good

In the time of Jesus, Rome was ruled by an emperor whose word was law. There was no democracy. It was a dictatorship. Yet when Paul, who lived during the time of the infamous and deranged emperor Nero, wrote to the church in Rome, Paul said that everyone was to submit to the governing authorities (Romans 13:1). He then reaffirms that those authorities are put in place by God. Rebelling against authority is rebelling against God and brings judgment on the person who chooses to rebel.

The government is supposed to be there to do you good, even when it asks us to pay taxes (which Paul tells us we are to pay).

I was a missionary for many years in countries very different from the one I was born in. These were places where the governments were anything but a democracy. I know what it's like to live under unjust governments and to wrestle with issues like immigration, maddening bureaucracy, and something as simple as trying to get a phone in my office. I've dealt with government officials who wouldn't do anything without a bribe, things that we would consider normal expectation of duty here.

We complain about taxes, and our country is far from perfect; but we have no idea how good our infrastructure is compared to other places. I would have gladly paid taxes to have a security system I could trust or roads and schools that were dependable. The core reason that so many nations are stuck in vicious cycles of poverty is because of the untrustworthy nature of those in charge of the wealth. The issue isn't money when it comes to taxes. The issue is trust, and when that begins to crumble no nation is immune from disorder and ever-increasing lawlessness.

I had a colleague on the mission field who, after many years of study, came to the conclusion that taxes were unconstitutional and that he would no longer pay them. That same man also had trouble with the principles of giving and tithing. Isn't that suspicious? Was it the taxes, or a lack of trust? Where does our money come from, anyway? And more importantly, who does that money belong to?

On our money, it literally says "In God We Trust." But we don't handle that money as if we do. By submitting to God's authority and those He puts in authority over us, what we're really doing is putting our trust in God.

Peter tells us that, for the Lord's sake, we should submit ourselves to every human authority. Why such a blanket statement?

We can't possibly all agree on how things should be. By submitting to human authority instead of fighting with each other for our version of right, we're acknowledging that we ultimately operate under a much broader kingdom governed by love, truth, justice and respect. We acknowledge that we trust God above every other power. If anybody would have understood how to live and even flourish within this tension, it would have been the first century believers!

> **BY SUBMITTING TO GOD'S AUTHORITY AND THOSE HE PUTS IN AUTHORITY OVER US, WHAT WE'RE REALLY DOING IS PUTTING OUR TRUST IN GOD.**

TRUST IS OUR FOUNDATION

Trust is when we set our hope and confidence on someone or something. It's when we lean or fall on them and they catch us. Trust is fragile. It's foundational to every relationship, but it's so easy to break.

Aren't dating relationships often about testing people checking them out, to see if they are trustworthy? There's typically no real commitment until we think someone is trustworthy. We make a date, we go out, and we keep a close eye on the other person. How do they act? What do they say? How do they treat others?

We're trying to decide if we should take the risk of allowing this person in closer. We're looking for clues that tell us our hearts will be safe with them. We're looking for character and consistency. Once we get engaged, we get serious about the relationship. Then marriage comes, and it's the ultimate commitment, a lifelong vow.

The deeper the commitment, the greater the level of trust we need. Think of a building. The higher the building goes, the deeper the foundation needs to be. I have seen that, in many parts of the world, houses are not necessarily built on any significant foundations. Now, you can build a structure without one, and it might even appear to work for a period of time. But when—not if, but when—the earth moves or the wind blows, a building that has no foundation has nothing to keep it in place. My wife and I have been married over forty years, and we've had a few storms we have had to weather together. With a foundation, the building much more likely to make it through and still be standing when the storm passes. No foundation means things tend to fall apart or even come crashing down when the going gets rough.

Temptation or trials don't automatically produce character in our lives, but they do a great job of revealing what is or isn't there.

Where we lived in Mexico was tropical, and everywhere you looked were palm trees of all kinds that thrived in that climate. One of the most majestic are called royal palms, and they grow upwards of eighty feet tall. They look like giant elephant trunks.

When a storm comes, those palms bend like crazy. But because of an incredibly extensive root system, they rarely ever break. They just snap back to attention after the storm passes. It's really amazing to see them in action in a strong wind. One morning, I was out walking and realized that the construction project at the university across the street had taken on a new look. There had been a few palm trees on the property before, but now they were renovating the campus landscape by putting in rows of newly transplanted 30-foot palm trees to line the entryway. I was curious as to how it was done, so I walked over for a closer look.

They were using a giant machine, similar to a backhoe, that dug huge, deep holes. They would haul in a young palm tree plant, drop it in the hole set upright, and then landscape all around it. It was like creating an instant paradise.

A year later, we had a small hurricane come through our region; and when I went out the next morning to survey the damage, I was surprised to see many of these palm trees down. Seeing one of the workmen handling cleanup at the site, I went over to talk to him.

"What happened to these palm trees?" I asked him.

He explained that the palm trees that survived the hurricane were the ones that had already been there. They'd had years to establish a broad, horizontal root system that could extend one hundred feet out from the base of the tree! That system went down into the earth and supported that tree so that when the wind blew, they bent but were not broken or uprooted.

Trust is like a root system when it comes to relationships.

The greater the commitment, the more significant that relationship is to you, the deeper and more extensively trust has to be developed. If this is true, then time is on your side. Pay attention to the speed at which things are moving. I am always apprehensive when I see trust being rushed or forced upon someone in a relationship because important signs will often be missed or ignored. The little things matter because so many of our everyday decisions affect our level of trust.

We Behave According to How we Trust

Trust is directly connected to how we act.

Imagine a woman is planning to go out on a first date. The man tells her to be ready by 5 o'clock because that's when he'll pick her up and take her to dinner.

She plans her whole day around that time, structuring how she gets ready so when 5 o'clock rolls around, she looks wonderful.

But then it's 5:15. And 5:30. Pretty soon it's an hour and a half later, and there's no one at her door. What do you think is going through her head?

She's hungry. Angry. Confused. Embarrassed. Was she forgotten? Stood up? Did he change his mind about her?

Finally, the man pulls up, offering a lame excuse about his dog and his car keys. Maybe she gives him the benefit of the doubt because it is possible he had a dog with a taste for keys.

But the next date, when he's supposed to pick her up at 5 o'clock, and he's thirty or forty minutes late, guess what? She's going to start thinking if this guy does this with time, makes a promise but can't keep it, where else in his life is he doing the same thing? Can she trust his word?

When we don't keep our word, violate a commitment we have made, or even indulge our selfishness a bit, we lose some measure of trust. And when someone loses trust in another, they instinctively begin to pull away.

We know we don't want to suffer. And people who can't be trusted are people who will likely hurt us if they are allowed to remain too close to us. It can be both wise and loving to back up and keep some distance between you and the untrustworthy person. It's how you keep them accountable for what they say and do. We are not looking for perfect behavior because that is unreasonable. What we do look for is consistent behavior, something we can depend on in the ups and downs of life. Whether we are looking for a mate, hiring a new team member, or starting a friendship, the principle remains the same: I want a life that is stable.

It's important to understand that trust is not the same as forgiveness and love. Forgiveness and love are hard choices we make towards another, while trust is earned, ebbing and flowing with a person's actions.

Love is powerful; we can choose to love the most obnoxious person in the world. We can forgive people who have hurt us deeply. We choose to make those decisions. Who hasn't witnessed the scene of someone getting carted off to jail for twenty years for some horrible crime, and his mother is there crying and assuring the world that he's basically a good boy? She loves him deeply, despite it all.

This can seem confusing, but I liken love and forgiveness to a simple light switch. It's either on or off. When you hurt or disappoint me, I either choose to love and forgive you or I don't; and we try to move forward from there. This can be challenging; but with God's grace, it is entirely possible. Otherwise, He would not have commanded us to love our enemies or to forgive seventy times seven. Trust, however, is like a dimmer switch that rises or falls with someone's behavior. This is why trust level is so critical to pay attention to. Oftentimes in a conflict, we want to forgive or be forgiven and maybe we even do; but trust can't just rush back in and demand a place. It is restored back to life slowly and carefully, and it becomes a critical part of the rebuilding process. When trust is fractured, that dimmer switch has some distance to travel before that light—the trust—is back to its full potential. Tom Marshall in his book *Right Relationships* identified four aspects of what makes up healthy and enduring relationships. He describes love as the most rugged, trust as the most fragile, understanding as the most difficult, and honor as the most neglected. Think for a minute about the deepest and most satisfying relationships in your life, and you will find that all four of these qualities will be operating in varying degrees.

Where We Put Our Full Trust

There is One Person we can put our full trust in: God.

Proverbs 3:5–6 tells us to trust in Him with *all* of our hearts, leaning not on what we understand but on Him. In everything we do, we should acknowledge Him and trust in Him; and He will make our path straight instead of confusing and crooked.

Notice that God wants one hundred percent of our hearts. *All* of them. Not ninety percent, not most of them, but all of them.

Our hearts are different from our heads. God isn't asking us to understand everything, which is what we'd use our heads for. He's asking us to completely trust Him, even when there are moments we don't completely understand.

Our current culture places a high value on education. It exalts intelligence and rational thinking, which are products of the Enlightenment. These are wonderful qualities that have fueled innovative research, mind boggling inventions, and incredible creativity. But have these advancements alone actually made us better and kinder human beings? God expects us to use our minds to their fullest capacities because He created us in His image to imitate Him. In so doing, we bring Him glory on the Earth. Our minds are magnificent things because God made them so.

But the writer in Proverbs is not calling for us to give God our minds. He's calling for our hearts, the seat of our emotions and affections, that hidden place deep inside of us, the fountain that our life flows out of. The Psalmist didn't ask God for a clear head; he asked him for a clean heart.

Consider a relationship where your head and heart aren't in the same place. You're operating on instinct with your heart flashing green, while your head is a flashing red light telling you to stop. God gave us both a head (intelligence) and a heart (an inner compass), and He's asking us to trust Him with all of it.

A lot of people wait to trust God until they've figured a situation out. They want all the answers or an explanation right now. They'll believe in creation or something spiritual if it can be completely explained to their satisfaction.

Who in the world would have such answers?

The desire to wait until we understand every question before we'll trust God can sometimes be a smokescreen for other issues. Deep down we realize that a sincere commitment to trust Him with every aspect of our lives has very real implications, and so we decide not to decide. It's funny how people won't pay attention to God until something tragic happens; and then suddenly it's the God we don't believe in who is now on trial.

"How could you allow this, God?" we say, demanding some sort of explanation for His behavior.

"I may not give you one," He replies. "Can you stop leaning on your understanding?"

In the ancient world, when kings appeared in public, they would often have a priest on one side and a sage or prophet on the other. It was a visual that said the king wasn't smart enough on everything to rule alone and that he leaned on both his confidants.

We can't lean on what we feel or what we think we understand.

TRUSTING GOD IN THE CLOUDS

We often find ourselves in a place where we are challenged to trust God. Oddly enough, that kind of trust can become more difficult the more educated or experienced we are. Many experienced pilots have made deadly errors because they became lax on safety and rules, thinking their flight hours would make up for a missing horizon in the clouds.

We all have some kind of instinct, an innate behavior that's different from a reflex. It's something we've learned over time, a way to respond. When we end up in a certain situation that we recognize, our instinct kicks in, for good or bad.

A woman raises her voice, and a man has an instinct to react a certain way that he learned from his past. The pastor starts talking about money, and people tune him out because they were burned in the past. A supervisor speaks to us about our workplace attitude, and all our defenses go up including thinking about an exit strategy. We have developed instincts for survival, for self-sufficiency, and for handling relationships. Instincts can make us desperate, especially if we're backed into a corner. They drive our behavior.

The pilots who made errors reverted to pure instinct. They flew by the seat of their pants, a reference to how you can feel the airplane turn based on how the weight shifts your backside on the seat. But not every situation is the same. Not every airplane or seat is the same. And flying by instinct in a situation where you can't see everything clearly is dangerous. Just as smart pilots rely on their instruments when visibility is low, we can learn to trust God's Word and character when our instincts or feelings have clouded things up.

The Word of God is a time-tested, calibrated instrument that claims to be steadfast and enduring through time and culture. Everything inside of us may be screaming that it's outdated, untrustworthy, antiquated, or old-fashioned; but at the end of the day, we find it's the only thing still standing.

From the very first page of the Bible, the enemy's goal has been to convince us that we can't trust God or take Him at His word. "Has God said?" whispered the adversary to the first couple.

When our hearts are familiar with God's character—because of time in prayer, time in His Word, and because we've exercised our faith and trust in Him on a regular basis, we become acquainted with how He operates, how He thinks, and what He does. We will begin to recognize whether or not advice or information we hear is in tune with Him.

> THE WORD OF GOD IS A TIME-TESTED, CALIBRATED INSTRUMENT THAT CLAIMS TO BE STEADFAST AND ENDURING THROUGH TIME AND CULTURE.

Trusting God instead of leaning on our own understanding is very difficult if we haven't put in the time to develop a relationship with Him. Doubt and fear will rage against our faith; and our adversary pits God against us, which then leads us to question His love and His wisdom for our lives. When you hang around seasoned or even battle-scarred men and women of faith, you will notice that trust is the defining characteristic of a disciple.

A Clearer Path Ahead

When we trust God and not our own smarts, He works on our behalf to make our path straight.

He didn't say it would be problem-free. He didn't say it would be smooth sailing. He simply said He would make our path straight.

Many times I've met with someone who I haven't spoken to in a year or so. We'll sit down and have coffee; and inevitably, they start up the conversation with the same conflict, the same offenses, the same attitudes—nothing has changed. They're having the same fights with the same people; or maybe they have a new job, and they're having the same problems at the new one as they did the old one.

We'll change leaders, churches, jobs, and partners; but we struggle with doing the hard work of changing ourselves.

When God says He'll make our paths straight, it means He won't keep us going around and around in a circle.

Ever find yourself traveling up a street when suddenly you encounter a traffic circle? A roundabout is a great way to intersect two roads and travel in different directions, unless you never leave the roundabout. Going around and around may give you the illusion of progress, but you're really not going anywhere.

The Israelites spent forty years wandering the same wilderness around the same mountain, going around and around. The straight path to the promised land was taken off the table because of their disobedience; instead, they got to do laps around Sinai. That same God would call His wandering people back to Himself again and again with the offer to "Come let us reason together," (Isaiah 1:18)

If we acknowledge God in both the little and big areas of life, He delights to work with us. We don't have to be problem-free to approach Him. He's simply asking us to recognize His right to reign in our lives so that He can stop us from wasting precious time going in circles.

LIVING IN TWO OPPOSING KINGDOMS

Christians are called to function within the systems that God has placed them in. We can't completely withdraw from the world. But to avoid making foolish mistakes and reacting in anger to the injustice and sin we see in the world, we have to develop practices that help us hear His voice amidst all the noise and rancor. This is not easy.

On social media, anger spreads the fastest.[18] Powerful emotions emotions—both positive and negative—capture our attention. But anger takes the cake. Of all the emotions we could express, that's the one that will go viral the quickest.

---

[18] "Anger Spreads Faster On Social Media Than Any Other Emotion." Fast Company, 17 Sep 2013, https://www.fastcompany.com/3017596/anger-spreads-faster-on-social-media-than-any-other-emotion.

In the kingdom of the world, with its addiction to information and activism, anger is the strongest currency.

I can go into a coffee shop and talk about nearly anything and not create a stir. I can talk about politics, religion, compare Christianity with Buddhism, talk about the environment, current events, news—and for the most part, people are willing to have a conversation and allow it to happen. But start speaking the name of Jesus out loud and people start getting uncomfortable. There is a tension you can almost feel, people either leaving or throwing glances in my direction.

That's often the tension of the two kingdoms rubbing up against one another—the kingdom of darkness (this world) and the kingdom of light (God). Everything about the real Jesus and His cross is threatening to the kingdom of darkness and sometimes even to those who call themselves His followers. The real Gospel is an equal opportunity offender. Timothy Keller describes it like this: "the preaching of the gospel is terribly offensive to the human heart. People find it insulting to be told that they are too weak and sinful to do anything to contribute to their salvation. The gospel is offensive to liberal-minded people, who charge the gospel with intolerance, because it states that the only way to be saved is through the cross. The gospel is offensive to conservative-minded people, because it states that, without the cross, 'good' people are in as much trouble as 'bad' people. Ultimately, the gospel is offensive because the cross stands against all schemes of self-salvation."[19]

---

[19] Keller, Timothy J. Galatians for you. Purcellville, VA: The Good Book Company, 2013.

Many of the old hymns of the church would focus on this world not being our home, that we're "just a passing through." We are surely passing through; but meanwhile, we are missionaries and ambassadors. We are salt and light, and we have work to do here. We are here to witness and testify, to share Christ, to love and be among people, and to become all things to all people so that they would be saved (2 Corinthians 9:22).

We live daily with this tension. We remain here to faithfully function for God's purposes. In turn, we cannot conform to the world's image. Living with this perspective, we come to realize that the Gospel message is the most subversive thing on the planet, and the confession "Jesus is Lord" is the one revolution that will endure when all the rest have run their courses. We have to be careful not to put too much stock into movements that ultimately don't lead to a change in the hearts of people. Real transformation is Gospel business.

WE ARE CALLED TO BE FOLLOWERS OF CHRIST

I knew a couple who were missionaries in a nation positioned near the border of Iran. Tens of thousands of Iranians would travel to this much-freer country on holiday to party and have fun. When I visited them, I watched as busloads of Iranians poured into the city looking for hotels and bars.

My friend told me that everywhere you went in the nation of Iran there was anti-American propaganda, from billboards to the radio. They were once in a hotel in Tehran getting ready to check out. In the hotel lobby was a display of flags of the nations, but one was missing. There was no American flag.

As they stood, waiting to check out, the manager came out from behind the counter and over to the couple. He took her by the arms and spoke.

"I hope you enjoyed your stay at our hotel," he said. "Did you notice our display in the lobby? All of those flags?"

"Yes," she said.

"Did you notice anything missing?" he asked.

"Yes, the American flag is missing."

"Do you know why the American flag is missing?" he asked.

"No."

Leaning in and whispering, he said, "Because I want you to know that we carry your flag in our hearts."

She was moved by what he had said, but he wasn't done.

"When you go home, you tell the American people that we love them, that we love what you stand for. That's not the message on the billboard, but we want you to know we love your country."

Everywhere they went in Iran, people would pull her aside and tell her the same thing. When she got home and shared the story in a church, a woman came up to her afterwards and admitted that, until she'd heard that, all she wanted was to see Iran judged. Her heart was changed by that insight into the lives of the real people on the ground. This is possible if we will take the time to listen carefully to people's pain instead of aligning ourselves with the raging mob.

There is certainly a place for resisting evil and oppression, but Jesus calls us to be humble followers first. That's the Kingdom of God.

So what are we supposed to do?

We must function in this system until God takes us out or puts us somewhere else. We are to seek the welfare of the city we've been placed in, without hating anyone in it, knowing that God's intention in putting us there isn't to harm us but to prosper us (Jeremiah 29:11). Many times, as a missionary, we'd move to a place and have to learn the system all over again. It was frustrating and maddening at times, but we had to learn to live there because that's where God had placed us.

This leads us to wondering where God is in the midst of this. Why doesn't He act more decisively? Perhaps a display of His wrath might help wake people up? The fact is that He acted decisively at the cross; and it was His mercy and humility on display there, not His power. That kindness is meant to lead us to repentance. Judgment rarely does. The cross is what settled the problem of our broken relationship with Him and in turn with others. The Just One paid the price for the unjust and made a way for us to begin living again. The cross is the manifold wisdom of God now worked out in and through His church. For millions of people over the last two thousand years, that was enough to cause them to lay down their lives for Him, to endure hardship and suffering, and to wait patiently for the fulfillment of all that He has promised.

DOING THE WORK

I often say there are four W's we should occupy ourselves with: wait, worship, work, and witness.

Waiting isn't something we are naturally good at. Some of the biggest messes I have made are when I wouldn't wait. However, this kind of waiting isn't a passive activity lived with our heads down. It's a living activity of prayer and seeing our world with ears and eyes wide open to what God is doing. I've found that the more I pray, the less I worry, criticize, complain, or do things that I later regret.

By worshiping, we acknowledge together a common creed that reminds us regularly where our allegiance lies, that we serve the King of Kings. By working and witnessing, we participate in seeing His kingdom come on the Earth in big and small ways. We work to bring justice where it is lacking, and we stand up for the oppressed and needy. We humbly but boldly bring truth to the public square, and we serve others sacrificially. We imitate our Redeemer by laying our lives down for one another in big or small ways; and no matter what our job or career is, we do it as if we're playing to the Audience of One. Regardless of the circumstances around us, we know who we are and why we are here. We are a resurrection community of life in what John Paul II called a "culture of death." The church is, as Eugene Peterson says, "where we practice resurrection … it's the workshop for turning knowledge into wisdom, becoming what we know"[20] The writer and holocaust survivor Elie Wiesel in his book *Night* recounts the story of how he and his fellow prisoners in a German concentration camp

---

[20] Eugene Peterson, Practice Resurrection: A Conversation on Growing Up in Christ (Grand Rapids: William B. Eerdmans Publishing Company, 2010), 138.

were forced to witness a young boy's execution by hanging. He had been accused of sabotage. The guards made everyone watch as the boy kicked and twitched in the throes of death. He heard a man standing behind him in the crowd say, "Where is a merciful God?" As they stood there, he asked again, "For God's sake, where is God? And from within me I heard a voice answer, Where is he? This is where—hanging from this gallows."[21] The question we so often hear thrown out is, "How can we believe in God?" However, I think it's fair to also ask, "How can we believe in man?"

Years later when interviewed near the end of his life, Wiesel was asked "Do you still have faith in God as the ultimate redeemer?" His response was "I would be within my rights to give up faith in God, and I could invoke six million reasons to justify such a decision. But I am incapable of straying from the path charted by my forefathers, who felt duty-bound to live for God. Without the faith of my ancestors, my own faith in humanity would be diminished. So my wounded faith endures."[22]

If we're citizens in the kingdom of God, yet living and functioning in a world that doesn't recognize that kingdom, how is it possible to participate in one without betraying the other?

---

[21] Elie Wiesel, Night, trans. Marion Wiesel (New York: Hill and Wang, 2006), 63–64.

[22] Aron Hirt-Manheimer, "On God, Indifference, and Hope: An Interview with Elie Wiesel," Reform Judaism 25, no. 2 (Winter 1996): 17.

Isaiah prophesied that Jesus the Messiah would come, and the government would be on His shoulders. Jesus claims to be the only wise and worthy God capable of governing over all people and all authorities, both visible and invisible. He has never made a mistake or acted unjustly. The One who invites me is not ashamed of His credentials, and as long as we are on this side of eternity, living by faith is everyone's lot. Saints and sinners alike all have to grapple with some measure of mystery.

CHAPTER TEN REFLECTIONS: REFLECT ON YOUR ALLEGIANCE

1) On my life journey, have there been times where I have wandered off the path of faith and found myself in a wilderness or going in circles? What did it look like?

2) Can I point back to the circumstances that enticed my heart to drift? What was God saying to me in those moments?

3) What lesson can I learn so I don't waste the experience, but instead make the most of it?

4) What practices and rhythms give life to my heart and soul? What things diminish me?

This Is Not the End

"Life is a short and feverish rehearsal for a concert that we cannot stay to give. Just when we have attained some degree of proficiency, we are forced to lay our instruments down."

– A.W. Tozer

"A good name is better than fine perfume, and the day of death better than the day of birth. It is better to go to a house of mourning than to go to a house of feasting, for death is the destiny of everyone; the living should take this to heart. Frustration is better than laughter, because a sad face is good for the heart. The heart of the wise is in the house of mourning, but the heart of fools is in the house of pleasure ... The end of a matter is better than its beginning."

– Ecclesiastes 7:1–4, 9 (NIV)

Here is a profound truth we can't afford to miss: endings matter. They matter a lot. So we better get them right.

One of the most famous novels of all time is Victor Hugo's *Les Misérables*. Clocking in at more than 1400 pages, it has been adapted for both film and stage. Having seen it in both those formats, there is one scene in the beginning that never fails to stop my heart. It's where a criminal named Jean Valjean is just released after nineteen years in prison for stealing bread. An angry and bitter man, he finds himself sleeping in the streets when he is taken in by the bishop, who offers him dinner and a warm bed.

Jean Valjean's instincts cause him to violate the bishop's hospitality, and he steals his silver. He's captured once again by the police. But the bishop, rather than demanding justice, offers him forgiveness and another chance at life. He not only gives him the silver, but he speaks a prophetic word over him.

He looks him in the eye and says "And don't forget, don't ever forget, you've promised to become a new man." Jean Valjean is dumbfounded by this act of mercy and stammers, "… why are you doing this?" The bishop responds, "Jean Valjean my brother, you no longer belong to evil, and with this silver I bought your soul. I've ransomed you from fear and hatred and now I give you back to God."[23]

Why do those kinds of scenes resonate so deeply with us? Because they are an echo of our deepest longings put there by our Creator. This has been the plot line of countless odysseys and epic adventures. We long for mercy to triumph over

---

[23] Victor Hugo, Les Misérables, trans. Julie Rose (New York: Modern Library, 2008).

judgment, for goodness to vanquish evil. We want the love story to come true.

In that moment, the bishop acted as prophet, priest, and pastor to him. This bishop saw something in him that no one else did. He didn't see a criminal forever trapped in his wretched past. He shepherded his soul and showed him this was not the end of his life. In a moment of stunning grace, a new ending was written. The bishop looked at Jean, really looked at him, and saw not a criminal, but a brother. And with a few words and a priceless gift, he handed Jean a blank page and said, "Start again, my friend. This is not the end."

This can be our story. Our past does not have to have the last word over our lives. God is in the business of second chances. You see, in God's upside-down kingdom, endings are not what they appear. They are not periods, but commas, doorways into new beginnings, new stories waiting to be born. The teacher in Ecclesiastes invites us to lean in close and listen to the whispers of wisdom that endings offer. They are the revealing light that illuminates the true substance of what came before.

Do you know what the most valuable resource in the world is? More valuable than gold or silver, than diamonds or real estate? A resource so coveted and so valuable that people would pay anything to have more of it? It's time. We would like to stop the clock and have more time. We can always make a little more money, acquire a few more things, or do one more deal; but time is the non-renewable resource that each one of us are given a measure of. There is simply never enough time to do or to be all that we feel we were meant to experience or become.

In the Ecclesiastes passage above, the preacher's words seem unusually harsh. Is the day of death better than the day of birth? Better to go to a funeral than a baby shower? Better to mourn than to party? How could that be true?

We have to remember that our writer is speaking in the context of the journey towards wisdom. He is simply observing the ways of the upside-down kingdom where wisdom is gained by paying close attention to things we would rather avoid. It's counterintuitive to think that by embracing discomfort and even hardship, we grow up and gain what is most valuable. He is not saying it's wrong to rejoice at the birth of a newborn child or to enjoy the feast and laughter with friends.

What he is saying is that in the long view of things, endings speak to us in a way that beginnings do not. That's because oftentimes the end of a thing reveals what the beginning conceals! Think about how many ideas we have had or decisions we made that at the beginning seemed brilliant but when tested over time in real life turned out to be less than ideal. Or how many government policies were judged by history to be short sighted or flawed? It's easy to boast in the beginning of a great return, but the end reveals what is actually delivered. Many games seem to be won in the exciting first half, but they are often decided in the last few minutes.

The critical fact is that, in the end of a matter, we will discover if the promise or the promise maker was trustworthy. The noise coming from the house of feasting is very attractive, but the preacher says you would be wise to take a careful look at the endings in our lives and listen carefully. The end reveals what we have truly lived for, truly trusted in, truly treasured, and what we truly hope in. That's where the wisdom lies.

So here's the invitation, dear ones. As you walk the winding road of your one wild and precious life, let the reality of endings shape your todays. Live with the end in mind, not in a morbid sense, but in a way that brings clarity and purpose to each breath, each choice. In the crucible of an ending, the gold is separated from the dross. The unshakeable is separated from the fleeting. We see with clarity what really matters, what really lasts. And along the way God graciously offers to be a faithful and true companion in our quest for a life that matters both now and for all eternity.

Choose wisely.

"The queen of the South came from the ends of the earth to hear the wisdom of Solomon, and behold, something greater than Solomon is here."

– Matthew 12:42

Acknowledgements

I want to thank all my leadership team at Church on the Hill. I couldn't ask for better companions in the journey. You have sharpened and shaped my life. To my friends at Story Chorus who worked patiently with me, thank you for getting this project across the line. To Wes and Paula and to all the LifeWorks supporters. You helped make this idea a reality. David and Peter, your attention to detail in the editing went far beyond the extra mile. To my COTH family. Serving among you has been an honor. And finally, to Jesus: "In whom are hidden all the treasures of wisdom and knowledge" (Colossians 2:3).

Author Bio

Bruce and his wife Linda are currently the lead pastors of Church on the Hill where they have worked for 25 plus years. Church on the Hill is a multi-site ministry in the Willamette Valley of Oregon dedicated to building healthy disciples and to serving the greater community outside the walls. Before coming there, they  served together, with their two sons, for 16 years as full time missionaries living and working primarily in Latin America. Their life long passion is discovering, developing, and deploying the potential of the emerging leaders of this generation. He and Linda have been married 45 years and have two sons, married to wonderful women, and one lightning smart grandson.

Made in United States
Troutdale, OR
10/13/2024

23720441R00139